GREAT BLACK MUSIC
Ancient To The Future

Art Ensemble Of Chicago
Great Black Music
Ancient To The Future

Written, compiled, and edited by Lincoln T. Beauchamp, Jr.
in collaboration with the Art Ensemble of Chicago

© copyright 1998, 2022 by Lincoln T. Beauchamp, Jr., & Art Ensemble Of Chicago Publishing All rights reserved.

No part of this book may be reproduced in any form,
by photostat, microfilm, xerography, or any other
means, or incorporated into any information retrieval system,
electronic or mechanical, without the written permission
of the copyright owner.

Reprint International Standard Book Number 978-0-944602-08-9
International Standard Book Number 0-944602-12-6
Library of Congress Cataloging-in-Publication Data:

>Beauchamp, Jr, Lincoln T., 1949
>a/k/a Chicago Beau

>The Art Ensemble Of Chicago
>Great Black Music
>Ancient to the Future
>Includes index

Art Ensemble banner created by Akosua Bandele
Cover design by Sara Ciarroni
Design and layout by L. T. Beauchamp, Jr. and Sara Ciarroni
Proof reader, Alix Mitchell
Photolith by Felix Mathew
Printed in Italy by Litografica Iride srl, via della Bufalotta 224, Rome

Special thanks to Willa Woolston for her copy editing assistance.

Special thanks to Anne Pryor, Lowell Thompson, DonAlonzo Beauchamp, Carrie Holt, Howard Watkins, Esther Jenkins, and Kudus Onisemoh for their hard work, and cooperation.

Our sincere gratitude to Isio Saba for use of his photo collection, without which, so many of these pages would have gone un-graced. - Beau & AEC

Special thanks to Sara Ciarroni, and Felix Mathew for assisting me in the final phases of this project. - Beau

Art Ensemble of Chicago
P. O. Box 53429
Chicago, Illinois 60653
Tel 1.773.536.2200 / Fax 1.773.536.2270
E-mail: artensem@enteract.com - Web Page: http://www.aeoc.com

L. T. Beauchamp, Jr. E-mail: boola@compuserve.com

TABLE OF CONTENTS

A Prolusion Cum Appreciation
*by Lincoln T. Beauchamp, Jr.
'Chicago Beau'*
9

Full Force: Ancient To The Future
by Kalamu Ya Salaam
15

Roscoe Mitchell
*by Lincoln T. Beauchamp, Jr.
'Chicago Beau'*
23

Adventure As Necessity
Since The Beginning
*by Lincoln T. Beauchamp, Jr.
'Chicago Beau'*
25

Malachi Favors Maghostut
*by Lincoln T. Beauchamp, Jr.
'Chicago Beau'*
27

Lester Bowie Interview Parts 1 & 2
*by Lincoln T. Beauchamp, Jr.
'Chicago Beau'*
35/45

Famoudou Don Moye Interview
Parts 1 & 2
*by Lincoln T. Beauchamp, Jr.
'Chicago Beau'*
53/59

Venting For Don, Luba, Ari, and Ken
*by Lincoln T. Beauchamp, Jr.
'Chicago Beau'*
67

Blues For Zazen
by Joseph Jarman
69

Joseph Jarman Interview
*by Lincoln T. Beauchamp, Jr.
'Chicago Beau'*
70

Larry Stevenson Interview
*by Lincoln T. Beauchamp, Jr.
'Chicago Beau'*
77

Reflections On Paris:
The Early Days of The Art Ensemble
*by Lincoln T. Beauchamp, Jr.
'Chicago Beau'*
81

Art Ensemble Of Chicago
by Mike Hennessy
83

Celebrating
The Art Ensemble Of Chicago
by Isio Saba
85

races places faces & asses
by hartmut geerken
89

Reflections Of Jamaica
by Don Alonzo Beauchamp
91

Praises From Friends And Colleagues
94

Odwalla, The Poem
by Joseph Jarman
96

Odwalla, The Music
by Roscoe Mitchell
97

Selected Discography
98

About The Author / The Contributors
100

Index
101

The Art Ensemble
And The Drum

Heartbeat Of The Afrikan Spirit

A PROLUSION CUM APPRECIATION

Lincoln T. Beauchamp, Jr.
'Chicago Beau'

When Lester Bowie approached me with the idea of doing an Art Ensemble book project, I didn't have to think about his proposal for long, not even a second. I have known the Art Ensemble for over twenty-five of the thirty plus years they have been together. And before I knew them personally, I had heard the music of Joseph, Roscoe, Malachi, and Lester in various aggregations when I was a teenager on Chicago's southside. They were among the local heroes which included activist, Phil Koran; musicians, Richard Abrams, Muddy Waters, Howlin Wolf, Billy Boy Arnold, Willie Dixon, Fontella Bass, Bo Diddley; and radio personalities Herb Kent, Lucky Cordell, and Pervis Spann 'the Blues Man.' As individuals they were a part of a vibrant city-scene, where music and dance was at the very core of the day-to-day rhythm of the Black community. The pre-Art Ensemble cats were deeply imbued with the spirit and emotions that are Black people. No wonder that they were to become messengers and hosts for the Spirit. Malachi Favors Maghostut has said:

'For sure each one of us has been visited by the Spirit. As for me, I think if the Spirit weren't guiding, I don't think I could do it. I don't think this mission is based on me entirely as a person.'

'Great Black Music' Ancient to the Future, is indeed a profound and accurate proclamation of the Black Aesthetic. This epigram of the Art Ensemble of Chicago encompasses all forms of Black artistic expression and communication, from ancient rites and rituals to sanctified pulpits; from the language of drums to rap; from la Conga to the Jitter-Bug. With great guidance and love from the Spirit, the pantheon of ancient deities, and the energy and example of our ancestors, the Art Ensemble has for more than three decades delivered unto their audiences musical, lyrical, and visual excursions, indeed, from the Ancient to the Future.

There are varying accounts as to the very early days of the group. AEC members have slightly different recollections, as do some of the people associated with them. I think varying accounts are interesting because different people interpret differently the significance of an event; and as we age, perhaps some details can become vague or even omitted. However, what comes through from each member is the passion and dedication to the Art Ensemble which has absorbed more than half of their lives. You will read each member's description of the early days and other experiences in his own words. So, although I know them, and have done research for this project, still the best way for this history to be recorded is from the recollections of those who have made it; and if some academics or other smarty-pants types want to dispute something, they'll have six long distance runners of music and memory jerking their cerebellum in six directions, out of key, and that includes me. The truest cognoscenti of the AEC may be those who have shared and collaborated with them artistically; included in this book are comments from some of those individuals.

In this book there are contributions from those who have worked closely with the AEC, or who have followed their career, individually or collectively. These contributions are from Isio Saba, who has booked concerts and photographed the group for more than twenty years; Mike Hennessey, who is well known for his biography of drummer Kenny Clarke, and is a top-notch piano player; archivist hartmut geerken, who recently released a tremendous book on the career of Sun Ra and his Arkestra; Bridgette Fontaine, with whom the AEC worked and recorded in the Paris days; and author Kalamu Ya Salaam, one of the founders of the New Orleans Jazz and Heritage Festival.

Each member has been interviewed by me. Some of the interviews are printed in full which is the case with Famoudou Don Moye, Lester Bowie, and Joseph Jarman. Roscoe Mitchell, who is at the core of every interview and essay because it was his group which evolved into the AEC, is more commented upon, than commenting himself. Malachi Favors Maghostut, the sagacious elder of the AEC, is reflective and ponderous, as he has always been.

Knowledge and education are foremost in the AEC concept. Knowledge means knowing your instruments, the music, and continuing to develop. It also means the exploration of sound, from screams to bicycle horns to bells to the howls of silence. It means Delta Blues, Bebop, Samba, Reggae and so on, with a thorough knowledge. The Art Ensemble has spent a great deal of time learning, re-learning, and continuing to learn. And they share, they educate, from the stage, on recordings, and in direct contact with people by doing hundreds of workshops, lectures and demonstrations around the world for the past thirty years. About learning Roscoe Mitchell said recently:

'Actually, it seems like now is the real learning period. It never stops. This is a good profession to be in if you want to work hard. It definitely requires a lot of work if you want to stay on top of it.'
As to education, Lester Bowie comments:

'If you ain't ready to travel, pack up your family, or pack up yourself and hit the road, you're in the wrong business. Because that's what music is about. It's about spreading knowledge and education, and re-education. It's about spreading.'

He further adds:

'We are not only entertainment, we are education, refinement, culture. We are the Art Ensemble, not a Jazz Ensemble. We are playing music intended to elevate your intellect. We want people to think. We want people to say, "What the fuck was that? Why did they do that? How does that relate to that Blues piece they were playing?"'

Besides being educators, the AEC has influenced many individuals and groups, and aligned themselves with other artists from various genres. Over the years there have even been a number of copy-cat ensembles. Some came into existence out of respect and admiration; others, like what happens so often in Blues, were parasites trying to capitalize on other peoples struggles, history and creativity.

Indifferent towards the negative, and firmly grasping the positive, the AEC has forged ahead collaborating with various artists on a multicultural and international level. They have done films in France: *Les Stances à Sophie*, and *Crescendo*. They have had their music interpreted by symphony orchestras, and they have extended the dimensions of the Euro-symphonic form. Famoudou Don Moye assembled drummers, percussionists, and chanters from Mali, Senegal, and the Americas to join with the AEC for an extraordinary tribute to the tradition of the drum in Black culture. They have merged energy with Sardinian folk musicians, Elena Ledda, and the Tenores di Bitti; and in the early days created with French singer and poet, Bridgitte Fontaine. With the Amabutho Zulu Male Chorus of South Africa, they toured, produced and recorded a phenomenal CD for the DIW label, *Art Ensemble of Soweto*.

Speaking of recording, the AEC catalogue contains over thirty authorized recordings, and there have been reported at least that many boot-leg and rip-off releases. To serve as a counter-balance to the unscrupulous and to take matters in their hands, the AEC created their own record labels, AECO, and ReRip Records. The idea of ReRip is that if you stole our music, or released some music that we didn't authorize, or ripped us off, we're ripping it back from you. Hence, ReRip.

All of the AEC's recordings are outstanding. The Nessa and Delmark recordings of the early years represent a quality of music which was even then virtually unparalleled; and it is easy to hear the direction which has made the AEC become an institution. The ECM pieces are gems, four in all, especially *Full Force*, which won Record of the Year, 1981 from Down Beat Magazine; Jazz Album of the Year, 1980 from Melody Maker; Record of the Year, 1980 from Stereo Review; and Grand Prix Diamant 1980 du Festival Montreux, Switzerland.

Later, in the early 90's, the AEC recorded for DIW of Tokyo, Japan a total of seven albums. The richness continued. One recording included pianist, Cecil Taylor, on *Dreaming of the Masters, Dedicated to Thelonious Monk*. The other six recordings, one of which is dedicated to

John Coltrane, are equally abundant as anything they've ever touched. Still however, nothing replaces witnessing an AEC concert.

Their recordings are extensive. Near the back of this book is an AEC discography.

* * *

In 1993 Joseph Jarman left the group. No one knows why except Joseph and the AEC. In the interview which is contained herein he did offer the following answer to the question: Was your separation from the Art Ensemble really a personal issue? He responded:

'Yea, it's a personal issue. Plus it's a vibration that I don't want to put into the universe. It's been put there enough already. Whether it's true or false from my perspective the energy goes into the blended energy of every living thing, and it will have some kind of effect. So rather than create effect based upon that information, I would prefer to create effect based on all of the wonderful, beautiful, positive experiences that happened. Any non-positive experience that happened will filter down, if necessary, to be reported upon. And you will come to your conclusion, you will realize something—this and that. I don't think any non-positive element can come in an objectively researched situation.'

I am one of those individuals who hopes that time will do as she often does, and bring about a new season for Joseph and the other AEC members.

* * *

As I stated at the beginning, in this book, AEC members speak for themselves. So, I am going to close and let the real reading begin, for this book is a dance, drum beats, and a swirling of rhythms. That's what the AEC is all about. Throughout this book, however, there will be different comments from me as well as others. I will leave you a few words from a great admirer and colleague of the AEC, saxophonist Steve Potts.

The Art Ensemble is one of the most important groups of the last part of the Twentieth Century, one of the most important groups in modern music because of certain musical and artistic innovations. Their thing is a whole situation: from musical to spiritual, to life itself. I consider the Art Ensemble the primary group of the last part of this century.

To give to people such a large, varied, and beautiful palette of creation; I can't think of any body else that's done that

The caliber of musicians in the Art Ensemble is outstanding. They are motherfuckers! I have to use that word. They are Motherfuckers! They are playing their asses off; and what they are playing is so important. The visual aspect of their presentation is as incredible as hearing them. When you hear them—the phrasing, etc. All put together, they are Motherfuckers!

The AEC are universal—cosmic—interstellar—back in the alley messengers. Cats from the hood, and for me that's where their greatness lies, in their connection with the peoples, playing the people's music, dramatizing the people's lives.

Art Ensemble of Chicago
Salutes
The Chicago Blues Tradition
European Tour, Summer, 1993

Top row L to R: Famoudou Don Moye, Herb Walker, Roscoe Mitchell, Frank Lacy, James Carter, Malachi Favors Maghoustut. Bottom row L to R: Amina Claudine Meyers, Lester Bowie, Joseph Jarman, Chicago Beau.

FULL FORCE:
THE ANCIENT TO THE FUTURE

Kalamu Ya Salaam

Halfway back down the road of the Art Ensemble, that's 1980, Kalamu Ya Salaam wrote this article for the Black Collegian Journal. The purpose was to inform and educate Black youth about the group and their message. I find it fitting that this should be the first piece in this book, because of its relevance to the community from which all of the AEC members come.

Jarman whirls the white vacuum tubing in a slow circle just above his head producing a 'wooing' sound, or perhaps Roscoe Mitchell blows long breathes into one end of a four foot bamboo cylinder which seems to be at least three inches in diameter, it turns out to be the most mellow flute ever heard, conjuring images of spiritual retreat beside a still lake, high in the Tibetan Himalayas.

When the Art Ensemble of Chicago plays, every genre of Great Black Music is voiced: African processional music, New Orleans street music, Blues, swing, bop, new music; and all of it is done with only a few pieces of rarely referred to sheet music. Their swaggering Kansas City style riffs contrast with their neo-bop themes, juxtaposed against delicate, dancing ballads in three/four time, which in turn are backed by intense high energy, collective improvisation—all in the course of one night's concert.

When the Art Ensemble of Chicago plays, each of its five members commands a space, creates an aura, operates from an area within which are located diverse percussion instruments. As noted by Roscoe Mitchell, the multi-reed player and percussionist in the group formed in 1969, many of their instruments are *highly original in the sense that there are no others like them*. Although the guys bought their gongs and things from a store, there were a lot of instruments that were constructed by the musicians.

But, even as their rhythmically regal music calls forth and draws on the irrepressible heart beat of African and African-American life rhythms, the music is more than simply horns and drums. The percussion of the Art Ensemble is polyphonic as well as rhythmic. From belaphones, the West African precursors of modern day marimbas and xylophones, to vibes; from families of gongs to tuned sets of bells. The percussion work has a distinctive melodic element whose striking resonance reminds of the way many Black painters use their colors brilliant and uncut, straight out of the tube, splashing it thick on the canvas. This music is bold enough to use a siren full blast in the middle of horn solos, or honking car horns that anyone might hear on any American street, especially in the African-American communities where such strident sounds are as ubiquitous as dirty urban air.

SPIRITS ASCENDING: The Art Ensemble of Chicago has raised the ante on the role of percussion in contemporary music, their deployment of a battery of wood, metal, and ceramic instruments is the fullest extension of the African sensibility vis-a-vis percussion happening on the planet. For them, rhythm is more than beat, rhythm is music; a music which, correctly used, can express the totality of human sentiments; joy, pain, trance, enlightenment. In most expressions of modern American music, percussion is either incidental or an addendum to the major thrust of the music; for the Art Ensemble percussion is the matrix from which spring all other elements.

Equally significant is their use of conventional instruments, particularly by the two reed players, Roscoe Mitchell and Joseph Jarman. Just watching them manipulate the various saxophones is a consciousness-raising experience. It is particularly broadening to witness them playing the bass saxophone. The instrument is too heavy to pick up and must be played at a tilt on its stand. Even more interesting than the instruments themselves are the different approaches Mitchell and Jarman have developed. Roscoe Mitchell is a structuralist who turns sound over and around; he both plays and 'plays with' notes, constructing solos of complex permutations which he enunciates with what may look like disinterest to the casual observer. Jarman, conversely, jumps straight for the jugular, ripping into his music with impassioned prowess. He raises his foot, dips his knees, shakes his head; at every moment his body language announces his involvement with the music. As a duo, they weave a complex carpet of woodwinds whose originality is refreshing.

Lester Bowie is the wings of the Art Ensemble; sometimes a dove, sometimes a hawk, sometimes a phoenix, but always rising/riffing above the ensemble, sending streamers of brass sound around the melodies much like a tie that binds or a ribbon which embellishes a beautiful rope—if you can hear that. Wearing a long white smock, not unlike the clothing of a baker or a doctor, Bowie provides both the belly laughs and the sensitive caresses with his amphibious trumpet style; part of the time his playing is brilliantly conventional, much like black sprinters who run the hundred in nine flat, other times he's out in deep water, bobbing and weaving, teasing as he fashions unorthodox, enthralling filigrees of brass music as sleekly playful as dolphins or jovial as Muhammad Ali in his prime improvising a knockout of befuddled opponents.

Malachi Favors Maghostut, the bass player, was born in Lexington, Mississippi, but reared in Chicago. A significant number of Black Chicagoans have Mississippi roots.

Thus, it is no mere coincidence of time and place that the urban Blues bawled/balled on/off Chicago's Southside; Muddy Waters and others swimming those streets transformed Delta acoustic Blues/dust to

Southside electric Blues/concrete—this is the milieu from which Malachi emerged.

Favors is the Art Ensemble's obsidian touchstone. His forte is a thick-stringed sound which ably carries the harmonic chords in the pianoless quintet. Regardless of whatever else is happening, Favors is hanging in dropping bass notes as sturdy as the bellow of ten brass tubas. Don Moye, the percussionist/drummer, rides the rhythm low, side to side with body buried deep inside a maze of percussion instruments. Only his painted face is visible, intermittently bobbing to the surface like a freshwater scuba diver. Moye's chops are awesome. He is confident, competent, comfortable whether sitting behind the traps, standing before the congas, or adeptly manipulating the various hand drums. This man is the energy center; the spine sewing the group together; a grinding wheel turning and shooting sparks; or maybe a turbo-jet blasting lift-off as the drums roll.

AS BEFORE, SO AGAIN: This is the Art Ensemble of Chicago and what they play is Great Black Music - From The Ancient To The Future. To call this music 'jazz' is to make a major mistake. This is no background noise for lustful purchases of female flesh, no come-on to buy another drink, and another drink. This is not what can be easily labeled, or pigeonholed. This is a lifelong commitment. It is a life in itself. Listen to Maryland born, St. Louis bred trumpeter Lester Bowie: 'If you're going to play music, you just play music or you die. No in-between. If you die, they just find your body on the street one day with your horn in your hands if it's still there. That's the way you go down. If a person wants to be a musician and they're not ready to make a commitment, they can forget it, stop, give it up. They should go do something else that would be easier on them. This is a very hard business. In fact, it's a very hard life to be a professional musician.' Especially hard if what you make is Great Black Music; covering it all, doing the whole number without benefit of sponsorship from the world of so-called 'serious' American music. One reason the Art Ensemble is ignored is precisely because their music cannot be duplicated: you can't listen to two records for twenty days, write out a couple of charts, call in a few studio musicians and do what the Art Ensemble does; you can't wake up one morning, hear it on the radio and play it in class two weeks later; nobody can copy this music. Similar music can be made, other musics can be created—but what you experience when you catch the Art Ensemble live is unique, singular: at once a reflection of decades of Great Black Music and simultaneously the expression of a synergistic synthesis of five specific individuals. Unfortunately, in America, unless or until white musicians can be found who can play a specific music, that music is dismissed as 'eccentric' or 'flamboyant,' but is hardly ever considered serious or accorded the respect due it. But what else is new? Our task today is for us as a people to acknowledge our own greatness; recognize, respect, and celebrate ourselves.

Not since collectively improvised melodies moving in fierce momentum over a shifting harmony, propelled by a wickedly off-center backbeat jumped off the banquettes and streets of New Orleans with a syncopated scream around the turn of the 20th century; not since European marching ensembles, civil war instruments and raw Black creativity were forged into the music that has since been identified with the birth of so-called jazz; not since King Oliver, Armstrong's musical mentor on trumpet, and the young Louis took those unrehearsed, impromptu tandem trumpet breaks which left their colleagues scratching their heads and had novice musicians searching for the 'secret' music that these dudes had to have somewhere; not since then has group improvisation been raised to such an exquisite level of tender power.

Not since the beginnings has there been a group whose music has, over a period of ten or more years, been so expansive in its influences, so African in its spirit, so African-American in its essence, and so uniquely identifiable. This is Great Black Music, phase 1980, and only the legendary Sun Ra and his Arkestra occupy a similar level of consistent group excellence.

From the Ancient to the Future, without artifice, strictly by dint of human will and creative expression, by disciplining the body, dedicating the spirit, by any means necessary.

The Art Ensemble Of Chicago. My, my, my.

Art Ensemble Of Chicago
and
Amabutho Male Chorus Of South Africa

Top row: Joseph Jarman, David Serame, Joel Eguabe, Max Bhe Bhe, Kay Nxumazo, Zack Nyoni, Thomas Mayo, Jonas Bube, Roscoe Mitchell. Bottom row: Famoudou Don Moye, Lester Bowie, Malachi Favors Maghostut.

'I think

that music is the highest science in the world.

We want to be as high into the music as we possibily can,

so we always try to stimulate the highest

thought that we can.

The thing about us is,

if we're being honest and trying to do

our best to keep this music as high as we can,

then we automatically elevate or expand people's thoughts.

It is definitely a mind-opener.'

Roscoe Mitchell

ROSCOE MITCHELL

Lincoln T. Beauchamp, Jr.
'Chicago Beau'

The sounds are out there in the universe,
it's up to the musicians to bring them in.
                                    Roscoe Mitchell

Inklings of creative genius began for Roscoe Mitchell in a Spiritualist church where his uncle presided. It was in this church and other such sanctified tabernacles that Roscoe Mitchell experienced the music and dance that renders men, women, and children helpless, and lovingly basking in the light of the spirits

'The music in the church really had the most profound initial influence on me.' And there were other influences. 'On the radio when I was coming up, you didn't have the music divided up. There was no station just for Blues or R&B, or just for Jazz or popular. The stations usually played some of everything, so I was exposed to all the different kinds of music. I never separated the music in my head, that's why I play in all styles, if you will, as I create. Nothing stays the same, the music changes from moment to moment, and from performance to performance. On no two gigs will the music be the same,' says Roscoe.

At Chicago's Englewood High School, Roscoe studied baritone saxophone and played in the school band, and later after the army, studied for two years at Wilson Junior College in Chicago. During his army years, from 1958 to 1961, Roscoe felt he was a pretty conventional player. 'I heard Ornette Coleman's music but I didn't understand just what he was doing. It wasn't until a bit later that I understood what was happening.' Shortly thereafter, Ornette Coleman among others would become key influences on Roscoe as an innovator.

Roscoe doesn't single out any individual as having dominated his thinking musically. 'I like what a lot of people do, that's my thing: Eric Dolphy, Ben Webster, John Coltrane, Johnny Hodges, Wayne Shorter, Don Byas, they've all had an effect on me.' In 1961, Roscoe joined pianist Muhal Richard Abrams' Experimental Band, which was the beginning of Roscoe's minting of new sounds, and forging alliances with others who shared a common vision of political, social, and cultural expression through artistic creation. In the case of Roscoe Mitchell, the artist must be separated from conventional terms usually invoked to describe certain music. Avant Garde, New Music, Free Jazz, Modern Jazz, even the word, Jazz, in the opinion of Roscoe Mitchell, is a misnomer when applied to his creations.

As a composer, he has utilized various elements of music to structure balance between the forces of other creative souls. An example would be his compositions performed by The Roscoe Mitchell New

Chamber Ensemble, which embrace the works of poet, e.e. cummings; *because, it's this, and dim*. Here a balance of literature, music, and culture is achieved. This is the type of work which challenges the categorizing efforts of the pedantic academia who seek to classify every piece of music that's ever been written or played; and every creative utterance from whichever culture. Collaborators with Roscoe in this project also represent a multi-cultural/multi-ethnic balance: Roscoe Mitchell, woodwinds; Thomas Buckner, baritone; Joseph Kubera, piano; Vartan Manoogian, violin. Here we have artists coming together from distinctly different ethnic backgrounds and environments.

Creating situations to create music has been an important endeavor for Roscoe. Recognizing the need for an organization that could unite and encourage creative interaction among artists, Roscoe served as a catalyst for the inception of the Association for Advancement of Creative Musicians, along with Muhal Richard Abrams in 1965. This organization, in its third decade, serves as a model world-wide for creative musicians. From it have emerged some of the most accomplished musicians of our time, among them being Anthony Braxton, Lester Bowie, Leroy Jenkins, Ed Wilkerson, Chico Freeman, Don Moye, Ajaramu, Kahil El Zabar, Steve McCall, and The Art Ensemble of Chicago, the major impact group that grew out of the Roscoe Mitchell Art Ensemble. Through Roscoe's efforts, creative music has been advanced upon listeners the world over. Mitchell used the AACM as a model for the Creative Arts Collective of Detroit, an Artists' collective he founded in Detroit in 1976 while living in East Lansing, Michigan.

The world is no stranger to Roscoe, nor he to the world. His music is played everywhere, either recorded or with his live performances. He has traveled extensively, and from 1969 to 1972, Paris, France was home. Roscoe relates: 'I feel another time is coming on like the Paris days, when the real creativity, not the commercial music so much, had a real place. I think the creative music is about to resume its place in the 90s and beyond.' Music goes through transitions. Much of what is appreciated in art has to do with the political and social climate. Perhaps America will awaken from its apolitical and anti-cultural trance of two decades and become re-energized.

And the creations of Roscoe Mitchell will play a vital role in the new awareness of the populace . . . like the Paris days.

ADVENTURE AS NECESSITY SINCE THE BEGINNING

Lincoln T. Beauchamp, Jr.
'Chicago Beau'

Thirty-five years ago, before fame, before Paris, before the realization of dreams, before being the Art Ensemble of Chicago, Roscoe Mitchell, Malachi Favors, Philip Wilson, Lester Bowie, and sometimes Leonard Smith (now Falah Tayanamuh), creative collaborators and co-dreamers, set out on music adventures across the United States. From New York to St. Louis to San Francisco, they seized the energy of youth, and put forth their message of music. In St. Louis they joined forces with BAG, Black Artists Group; and ongoing was the constant flow of concerts in Chicago with other members of the AACM.

In 1967, armed with a couple of cartons of the LP, *Sound*, Roscoe Mitchell, Lester Bowie, and Philip Wilson, drove from Chicago to the San Francisco Bay area in Lester Bowie's metallic emerald green Bentley, with no pre-set concerts, or accommodations. They placed themselves in the bosom of fate. And as fate would have it, they ran into Roscoe's friend, Blues singer/writer, Nick Gravenitis, who offered them a house in which to live and rehearse in Mill Valley. Concerts were quickly organized in storefronts or other impromptu venues. Sometimes they would sell LPs, sometimes not. But the message of the 'new music' was getting heard. Roscoe, Lester, and Philip were breaking new ground, and influencing musicians from other genres. Coming around the house sometimes were Paul Butterfield, Elvin Bishop, Mike Bloomfield, Buddy Miles and other musicians who became the Electric Flag. Philip Wilson eventually joined Paul Butterfield's Blues Band.

Again in 1968, with the LP, *Conglipitous*, in tow, Roscoe, Malachi, and Lester headed for California. This time, courtesy of jazz enthusiast, and friend, David Wessel, they found lodging in East Palo Alto, a Black town much like East St. Louis, Illinois. No sidewalks, but a roots town teeming with the creative life force and spirit that is Great Black Music. Lester drove his motorcycle, a BSA Thunderbolt 650, Malachi and Roscoe drove Malachi's VW van across the country. This group, the Roscoe Mitchell Trio was the nucleus for the Art Ensemble of Chicago. To be added was Joseph Jarman, and later in 1970, Famoudou Don Moye.

The adventure of music and living, delivering the message by any means necessary, has since the beginning been at the core of Art Ensemble motivation.

Note: The full adventures are forthcoming in another volume.

'I know that Black people are very, very creative people. I believe that due to events way before you and I ever came about, events like slavery covered up these creative aspirations. Here we are, in a sense, giants, but we have become dependent because of all the negative things that have happened to us. What I would like to see the music do is help to rid Black folks of this dependency.

The spirit of music can do this, if you can get people to listen. The problem with getting Black folks to listen is that they are controlled more than any other people. But that's due to our background. Radio and television could control people to the degree that they don't use their thinking powers. We feel that our music deals with the mind. We're living in life, so our music is a reflection of the many phases of life. The chattel slavery that our ancestors went through still affects many of us psychologically, therefore hampering our ability to differentiate the good from the bad. In this state one is easily controlled by the media or any other vehicle that deals with the thought process. Case in point: Some years ago when the Board of Education in Chicago dropped music from its curriculum in inner-city schools, there was not a beep or a bop from the Black Community. We all see what shape our schools are in today.'

Malachi Favors Maghoustut

MALACHI FAVORS MAGHOSTUT

Lincoln T. Beauchamp, Jr.
'Chicago Beau'

Contemplative and sagacious, Malachi, the eldest Art Ensemble member, spoke with me about the group, its mission, and his chosen path.

April 1997, Modena, Italy

On the roots of his sprituality

When I first realized myself, I believe that I was in church, and the church was the Church of God in Christ. The Church was founded in 1897 by Brother Mason, as he was called in those days. Today throughout the world he is known as Senior Bishop Charles Harrison Mason, Chief Apostle of the Churches of God in Christ. So congratulations to the church on its centennial year.

I come from a line of preachers in the Church; cousins, uncles, and nephews. Until this day, my father, Dr. Isaac Favors was the most noted of pastors after the passing of his brother, Dewitt. He passed on in 1987.

The Mother Church is located in Lexington, Mississippi, where both sides of my family were natives. When the Church was organized my family became members. My mother would often tell us children that whenever Brother Mason would come to Lexington, he was always a welcomed guest with her family, the Mayfields.

Bishop Ford, who was one of the presiding Bishops of the Churches of God in Christ, stated in Jet Magazine in the late fifties that the late senior Bishop Mason was inspired by God through the Bible to continue some more of our African traditions of praise to the creator which had been lost during slavery.

The Church of God in Christ brought with it in its praise the use of all musical instruments: tambourine, guitar, you name it. Also in the praise there is testifying, singing, dancing, shouting, clapping of hands, speaking in tongues, and great congregational praise. They completely turned around praise in this hemisphere.

Just a footnote. My uncle, Brother Walter Mayfield was the Sunday School superintendent at Mason Temple Church of God in Christ. The headquarters of the Church were located in Memphis, Tennessee, for many years under the auspices of Senior Bishop Mason.

The first musical instrument that I ever heard played was the guitar, and that was Elder Utah Smith. He was my first idol. Everybody that picked up a guitar in the Church tried to sound like Elder Utah. The man was powerful. He could sing. He had a big baritone voice and he didn't need a microphone.

Then there was Elder Ruesaw. When the shouting went up in praise, he went into his free spirit dance. In my life I have seen great dancers in person, or in the movies, like Bill 'Bo Jangles' Robinson, Baby Lawrence, Teddy Hale, The Barry Brothers, The Step Brothers, The Rimmer Sisters, Fred Astaire, and great African dancers. There was no better dancer that Elder Ruesaw.

Elder P. R. Favors, who was one of the first Deacons at the Mother Church in Lexington, Mississippi, also organized the Third Church of God in Christ that was formed in Chicago, Illinois. The church was located at 1323 Blue Island Avenue, and later moved to 1319 13th Street. Some of his members included Sister Rosetta Tharpe, who sang and played steel guitar, along with her mother who sang and played the ukulele. Sister Rosetta Tharpe became famous in the fifties. And also there was the Gay Sisters singing group, and Mother Freeman, the grandmother of Chicago's great saxophonist, Von Freeman.

Like in Lexington where the Mayfields accommodated the Senior Bishop, Elder P. R. Favors home which was located on the Southside of Chicago, was the headquarters for Bishop Mason whenever he came to Chicago and the surrounding area in the 20s, 30s, and into the 40s.

The Spirit of the music has always been a part of my being, but did not manifest itself until I was in my late teen years. Then I awakened to GREAT BLACK MUSIC!

On the inception of the AACM, and the Art Ensemble

I was part of the original group, I was not one of the founders. The founders were Muhal Richard Abrams, Phil Koran, the late Steve McCall, and Jodie Christian. I came to the first meeting of the AACM at Phil Koran's house. Muhal called me up to the first meeting. I remember, in fact, I was the first Sergeant-at-arms.

Let me get back to something here and straighten something out. I spoke with Alvin Fielder just a couple of weeks ago. He was the original drummer with the Roscoe Mitchell Quartet. He remembers when we began. We made a recording which has not been released as of yet with the original Roscoe Mitchell Quartet. That group consisted of Alvin Fielder, drums and percussion; Fred Barry, trumpet; Roscoe Mitchell, saxophones; and myself on bass. That was the original Roscoe Mitchell Quartet. Fielder said we began in 1963, and this recording was made in 1963. We still have the master tape, and some day it will be released. This recording is the first recording of the Art Ensemble or any other AACM group. It was recorded over at the radio station at the University of Illinois. So, the Art Ensemble began as the Roscoe Mitchell Quartet in 1963. I always figured we had been going longer than a year when Lester came in 1965.

On moving to France

I wasn't for it at all. The cats had to coax me into going. First of all I don't like planes. Second of all, I just felt that the music should stay where it is, and people should come and check out the music where it originates, which never really would have happened because of the poor interest in our community.

And let me back up a little. It was some years ago I was standing out in front of McKies nightclub down on 63rd and Cottage Grove in Chicago. Memphis Slim was standing there, and this was before the Art Ensemble or any of that had come into existence. And Memphis was saying: 'I'm getting ready to go to Europe. I'm moving to Europe.' I said to myself, why would he want to go to Europe? At that time, Chicago had the greatest entertainment section in the world, right there on the Southside. When I first started playing, it was almost ten years before I ever really went off the Southside working. There were so many joints just on the Southside alone. And to verify this, just about six or seven years ago, we were doing a gig with Chaka Kahn, and Chico Hamilton was on the gig. And we got to talking about Chicago. Chico said back in the forties and fifties Chicago was the place. You couldn't top Chicago for the music. And this is the reason I couldn't understand Memphis Slim making that statement. But when I got to Europe and checked out Memphis Slim in his Rolls Royce, I never would have thought it.

I remember about a year before we went I looked at my horoscope, and my horoscope said that I was going to be on a ship and I was going somewhere way away. I said they ain't talking about me. Man, in a year's time I was on a ship going overseas.

Lester was getting ready to pack up, buy a trailer, and take the music on the road cross-country. Then the French drummer, Claude Delcoo, wrote the AACM and said he wanted to bring the music to Europe. Well, we didn't have any money, but Delcoo said if we could get there, he would get us some gigs.

Joseph was the first one to bring the message in that we were going over to Europe. We was in an AACM meeting, and after the meeting was over, Joseph came and said, 'We going to Europe!' Cause Lester had said he would finance the trip and we would pay him back.

Well, after we got there I found Paris to be pretty interesting and exciting. I was amazed at them narrow streets. Some of those streets I notice are one-way today. But back then they were two-way, and it was the funniest thing to see cars trying maneuver in two directions down those narrow streets.

On the scene in Paris

On the music scene I got to meet a bunch of cats that I had just heard of or read about. Cats like Philly Joe Jones, and Archie Shepp; I got to record with both of them.

Then there was the Chat que Peche. The majority of the Black musicians hung out at the Chat que Peche jazz club. Some of them cats down there were pugs, man, they'd fight quick. In fact it got to the place that they had an article in the paper which warned the French about the Chat que Peche, because of the rough and tough musicians that were hanging out there. Man, there were rough cats hanging out down there: Philly Joe, Sunny Maurry, Reverend Frank Wright; and you know he was rough. They was Joe Louis, Muhammad Ali, anything you wanted to call. You couldn't step out of line. They went over to Georgakarokos's office (BYG Records) and turned it out over money owed them.

On the the arrival of Famoudou Don Moye

Roscoe and Joseph and myself, we had a gig at the American Center in Paris. And we

were setting up the gig, and all of a sudden this congo player came up and started setting his stuff up. I think Roscoe asked me if I knew him. I said I didn't know him. I asked Joseph if he knew him and he said no. It was Moye. They asked me if I wanted him to play. I said OK, because I had played with a congo player when I was with Andrew Hill back in Chicago. And when we couldn't get a drummer we used a congo player, a dude named Pepe Brown. Afterwards I thought, yeah this cat sounds good. Then later Joseph said that he played every Tuesday down at some joint with Mal Waldron, and he plays traps. During that time we were looking for a drummer. We had a drummer a few years back, Phillip Wilson, and he left and went with Paul Butterfield's band. From then on we didn't have no drummer, and it come the time that we wanted a drummer. So I went over to this club, and there Moye was playing with Mal Waldron. I asked would he come out, we were looking for a drummer, and he said yes. And that's what happened, he came out, and that's the beginning of Moye.

On being a part of the Art Ensemble

I feel blessed that I got with the Art Ensemble, because I know I'm playing with some chosen brothers; otherwise how would we be together thirty years. Everybody can't do this. There are few of us musicians left who play what I call 'truths in music.' You can't be an exact vehicle for the word through your horn all the time because you're still human. But it's very few of us left that even to a degree, let that happen. As they say in the church, 'Let the word come on out.' However it comes, that's what happening. However it strikes you. And I'm glad to be a part of that, although I still bow down to all of my favorites: Dizzy, Coltrane, Parker, Christian.

On some memorable moments

One of the performances that stands out in my mind was the recording of *Baptizm*. I remember we were in Ann Arbor, Michigan, in 1972. There wasn't a cloud in the sky. I mean the spirit was there. It wasn't the only time, but that time really stands out. When we came off the bandstand Muddy Waters was getting ready to go on. He said, 'I don't know what yal was doing, but yal was *doing* it.' After that, Muddy Waters went out there and smoked! We became friends after that. The last time I saw Muddy we were in Montreal playing at Doudoo's joint. Muddy came by and checked us out. You know a lot of cats say they dig you just to be polite. But Muddy really meant it. So we became good friends. Another cat that used to come to our gigs was Master Horn Player, Rashaan Roland Kirk. To have great musicians like Muddy and Rashaan appreciate what you are doing is really encouraging.

On the possible destiny of the music

I know the Art Ensemble can survive out here. It seems that the people today are more interested in fairy tale music. When I say fairy tale, I mean what they singing about ain't really happening in life. That just means that they need something else other than what they are singing about to make something happen. That's the great imbalance in our culture. You got to dig deeper into the spirit, soul, and the meaning of life to come up with something besides, 'I love you baby.' To sing, 'I love you baby,' all the time to me ain't what's happening. Ain't no man supposed to be into that no way; you know what I mean? I find that's what's wrong with society, too much make believe. Our ancestors sang about their surroundings and family, etc.

I feel privileged to be in creative situations where we can strike up and play, and our ability to do this. Everybody can't do this. There are great musicians who can't do what we do. They don't have the inner ability or the vision to do it. And however it goes, I've heard musicians say that if they had the inner ability to do it, they would be bad. If they had the thing that we have to let them get away from what they've learned, and go on and try to create on the spot. Some people would really be bad.

A lot of great musicians don't know what they're missing by not furthering their musical spirit. You got to have the spirit of music to do this. Also, one must have a pretty good awareness of their cultural background; that helps them feel and see into the music of their ancestors.

Some of those who have affected my life in Great Black Music

Paul Robeson, Marian Anderson, Mahalia Jackson, Duke Ellington, Louis Armstrong, Art Tatum, Charlie Christian, Charlie Parker, Dizzy Gillespie, John Coltrane, Bessie Smith, Muddy Waters, James Brown. If I heard all of the music again that I've already heard, I believe I would be so enlightened that I would just fly away.

The music speaks! There is a message in the music for you.

'One of the immediate goals of our music is to stimulate thought. The main thing is to make the world a better place to live in, to make people able to function better together and really elevate their whole existence.

Music is the key to understanding. Music is a sound that stimulates very organized thought. It makes you think about everything. You start thinking about yourself and once you get people thinking, they think of many things. They think of how to make a better mousetrap.
Music can open people's minds up.'

Lester Bowie

LESTER BOWIE INTERVIEW - PART 1

Lincoln T. Beauchamp, Jr.
'Chicago Beau'

Lester Bowie and I meet in Paris in 1969, at the same time I meet the other members of the Art Ensemble of Chicago. On many nights we've enjoyed fine Havana cigars and talked about good times past, and those that lie ahead. Finally after years of talking and a freighter of cigars, I've managed to tape a conversation with this wonderful friend and genius.

September 1990, Chicago

Chicago Beau: Bowie. You're famous now. How did it begin?
Lester Bowie: I ain't *that* famous. Shit, if you famous you supposed to have some kind of cash. I may be a bit well known in some areas, but I ain't famous (laughingly). My father was a high school band director. He played trumpet. All of his brothers were brass players, his father was a trombone player, so it just kind of came in the family. My brothers are all professional musicians and ever since I can remember we've all been playing music.

Chicago: Where did yal come up at?
Lester: I was born in Maryland, but I come up in St. Louis, Missouri.

Chicago: So, most of your musical youth was in St. Louis?
Lester: Yeah, all of it. I was in St. Louis from the time I was about two years old up until I left to join the military. I was born in '41, so in the mid fifties was my real musical youth.

Chicago: How many were in your family?
Lester: I got two brothers, Byron and Joe.

Chicago: No sisters?
Lester: No sisters. We didn't allow no bitches in the house except my mommy, that was the only one. We couldn't stand girls—it was weird though. You know sometimes cats don't like girls. We even named Joe before he was born. Wasn't gone have no girl (big laugh). Now, for somebody who didn't like girls, I got four daughters and a granddaughter.

Chicago: That's what you get.
Lester: Yeah, that's what I'm saying.

Chicago: What section of St. Louis did you grow up in?
Lester: Well, the Black section. When I came up we didn't see many white people. I was about fifteen before I knew any white people.

Chicago: In your youth, did your father take you around to clubs?
Lester: What happened was I had a band at fifteen. At fifteen I was a professional musician in the union.

Chicago: What styles were you playing?
Lester: Dixieland, Boogie Woogie and R&B type stuff. Actually during that time I worked a few gigs with Chuck Berry around '54- '55. We worked a lot of shows people were having; high school dances, talent shows, that type of thing.

Chicago: Did you work over in East St. Louis, Illinois?
Lester: No, not until later. This is the first period I was playing. We played mostly in a teenage kind of setting. Later, after I joined the military and came back, that's when I started playing with Oliver Sain, Little Milton, Albert King and all those cats. I played in East St. Louis almost every night then. It was the hang.

Chicago: What branch of service were you in, what year did you come back?
Lester: I was in the Air Force and I came back around '61 or '62; it was in the early 60s.

Chicago: In the Air Force were you a part of the orchestra or band?
Lester: No, I was in the police. See, when I came through, I auditioned for the band and they said they didn't have any openings for a trumpeter in the band, but I could be in the bugle corps. I was given a choice of being in the bugle corps or the police. At that time I couldn't stand bugle corps; I thought that was beneath me because I had played in a concert band, solo cornet. So I wasn't gone play no one-valve bugle; that was for simpletons. So, I rather be with the police force and play with them guns, and get to hit me a couple white boys upside the head. I used to be def on them white boys. So I spent that time in the police. During that time I was also involved with a band. I had a regular gig with a Blues band in town [Amarillo, Texas].

Chicago: What was the name of the band?
Lester: I can't remember the name of that band, but the guy that ran the band, his name was Topps. Had the sweetest press-role I've ever heard and he had a hell of a shuffle. He could shuffle his ass off and his role was pretty like Art Blakeys.

Chicago: So, yal was just playing stomp down Blues?
Lester: Yeah, just stomp down Blues in Amarillo, Texas. I joined the service to travel and ended up spending all my time in Amarillo.

Chicago: After Amarillo, you went back to St. Louis?
Lester: Yes, then I went to school. During the time I was in the service, that's when I decided to become a full-time musician. Because before I had been playing a long time, I had been a professional . . . doing union gigs. I was a pro from fifteen, that's when I first started paying union dues. Give the cat [union man] ten dollars every time he catch you. I decided to go ahead and play music while I was sitting up in jail in the service. I was in solitary confinement.

Chicago: What were you in there for?
Lester: I was in there for whuppin a white boy's ass. I had shot up the barracks shooting at this white boy. They had got me for attempted murder.

Chicago: It was as a policeman you did this?
Lester: It was as a policeman. The service was some of the biggest fun I've ever had. It went the whole gamut: from police to prison. It was a great experience, it really got me focused. I learned how to get organized which is real important out here. Some of what I learned in the military, like organization and discipline has become basic in dealing with the music. You have to understand that discipline is important. Everybody in the Art Ensemble is a veteran except Moye. And that's been basic in us being able to be together all this time. We've lived in barns and tents and out in fields just like in the army. If we hadn't been able to know how to bivouac, we never would have survived.

Chicago: A lot of Black folks around my age were repulsed at the idea of going into the military during Viet Nam, fighting for white folks' wealth and ideology. I realize that during your military period there was much going on in terms of war, but your music and life are quite contrary to the images one has of a staunch patriot. Would you shed a little light on that for me?
Lester: Well you see, that has nothing to do with training. You see the military is good just for the training. Plus I had a ball. It was great. I wanted to get away from home. My choices were getting a job, go to college or join the military. I ain't had to get no job yet. I ain't interested in having no job at all.

Chicago: I heard that.
Lester: For me the military was adventure, man . . . a motherfucker getting to go out on his own. I learned how to get that good pussy and out there fucking, drinking and gambling and shit. I mean I learned all the things in life that you be reading about but you don't get to do as a kid. All of a sudden I'm smoking cigarettes, weed and stuff; plus I was the police too. To me that was a whole lot more interesting than going to college. But I wouldn't been in there during Viet Nam.

Chicago: You were so close to Mexico, did you play at all with Mexican musicians.
Lester: No, didn't even take the horn down there. All we did down there was drink and fuck.

Chicago: How old were you when you got out of the military.
Lester: Twenty-one. I was in there three years and seven months.

Chicago: So, with a lot of new experience under your belt, you headed back to St. Louis. Then what?
Lester: Like I said before, being in the military taught me some discipline; cause before that I had no idea what I wanted to do. I learned about winning and losing, about a lot of things. So, I got all that out of my system.

I made my decision while I was in solitary confinement—I was already in jail. I got busted again while already in the jail, that's how I ended up in solitary confinement. Two weeks in what they call the black box. No light and just a slot where they slipped your food in. In this box is where I got my shit together, because I didn't have nothing to do but sit there and think.

Chicago: What was your total confinement time?
Lester: It was around four or five months.

Chicago: So, your initial beef was shooting at a white boy?
Lester: It wasn't malicious or anything really, but this white boy from Tennessee took my seat in the T.V. room. So when I asked him about it he came out of his southern bag: 'Yeah I took your seat, so what' he says. Well, I ain't never been afraid of white folks. A lot of people [Blacks] got that fear built in, but I don't. So, I grabbed him by the collar, pulled him down, pulled my gun, and fired off four or five shots right next to his head and said:

'Motherfucker, if you ever think about saying some shit to me like this again, I'll blow your head off.'

This cat was begging.

'Lester, please don't kill me.'

So for that, they thought they was punishing me, but they was really helping me. It was another experience. I got to check out the appeal process, the lawyers, the jail time and so on. Nice experience. And it was giving me resolve. I thought to myself, whatever I'm doing must not be that hip cause it's led to this black box, and I don't want to see no more of this box. Everything I thought I must have wanted to do was a mistake. So I decided to get serious and be a full time pro in music. But I knew I didn't really play that well to be a pro. I wanted to be a Jazz musician and I knew I didn't know enough songs or anything. So, when I came out of the service I went to Lincoln University for a year in Jefferson City, Missouri. While I was there I was also playing in a Blues band. I've played in Blues bands all my life. That's how I made my living. I'm a pro and wanted to work and the Jazz gigs weren't paying nothing; I just did them for fun.

Chicago: You've got a real deep feeling and love for the Blues.
Lester: Oh yeah, I'm a Blues cat actually. When I came back I played with a cat called Jack Harris and the Invaders. We played the central Missouri Blues circuit.

Chicago: This is when you were at Lincoln?
Lester: Yeah. Check this out. The head of the music department called me in one day about me playing with this Blues band. He says to me that as a student of Lincoln University's Music Department, he didn't feel that it was appropriate for me to be playing in a Blues band. I told him to kiss my motherfucking ass. I told him to get the fuck out my face cause I make my living playing this damn horn. And that I ain't no seventeen year old motherfucker just coming out of high school, don't tell me what the fuck I should be playing. He did get to me, and even at this time, I don't care too much for

church people and scholarly types, people like that. There are some church people that I like personally, but what the Black church has stood for I don't agree with at all. These people, the educated people, the Black educators; these people shun the Blues. They call Blues the Devil's music, and bad. Well, the Blues is our deepest culture . . . these notes that the Blues singers is singing go back hundreds of years. And these are Black people supposed to be educated, you dig, against the real Black music. To this day I have mostly disdain for church people and the church philosophy and middle class Blacks. I really don't like them kind of people at all. *Ebony* magazine type motherfuckers . . . you have to hold me back sometimes. I think these kind of people have done a lot to thwart the advancement of Blacks because they are anti-cultural. Anytime you take your own creation and say it ain't shit in lieu of some motherfucker that's playing Mozart or some shit. . . . The same cat at Lincoln once before wanted to expel me for practicing Coltrane. I was playing some diminished chords you know. Then this cat fell up talking about that ain't your lesson.

Chicago: How long did you last at Lincoln?
Lester: I was there for a year. But I was there for just one thing though. There was this great teacher there named Marshall, a trombone player. Ironically he wasn't the head of the music department, he was the band director. He was a hell of an instrumentalist. The only reason I went was to take lessons from him, cause I wanted to be a pro so I knew I had to go into a period of intense playing. So, I never went to classes, I never bought a book. I just went to my trumpet lesson and practiced twelve, fourteen hours a day. I did my gigs and that was it. I was really poor. Then I went to North Texas State for a year because they was suppose to be so hip in Jazz. A white boy Jazz school. I learned how racist Jazz can be. These motherfuckers are down there studying Black music; you can degree in Black music down there, right—and Black people don't even like the stuff; and you got white folks in Texas offering the shit as a course you can get a degree in and they got nerve enough to be racist down there; and they studying Black music. They see the benefits of it, but still want to dog us. They don't want to give nothing up. So I went to school just to study and practice. I had no intention of ever finishing. I just wanted to get good enough to go on the road.

Chicago: So that was it, two colleges?
Lester: That was it, good bye. Then I started working with Albert King, Oliver Sain, and married my first wife during that time.

Chicago: What was her name?
Lester: Fontella Bass. She was singing with Oliver Sain at that time. '63, '64 around in there. Then I started working with Oliver.

Chicago: How many children did that marriage produce.
Lester: Four. Two girls and two boys. And I got two more girls with Debbie (current wife).

Chicago: After the hook-up with Fontella and Oliver, how did yal end up in Chicago?

Lester: What happened was Fonnie (Fontella) started recording for Chess Records. Her and Bobby McClure had a record out called 'Don't Mess Up A Good Thing.' So, she was working quite a bit around Chicago. Then after she made 'Rescue Me' and that started moving pretty good, then we moved to Chicago. This was around '65.

Chicago: You wanted to be close to the studio?

Lester: Yeah, and be close to the cash.

Chicago: Did you play on some of those Chess sessions with Fontella?

Lester: Yeah. And after 'Rescue Me', I became her musical director. That's when I really got a lot of experience leading bands. Now by me being Fonnie's musical director, I got to be with a lot of different bands like Jackie Wilson's and Jerry Butler's. If they wanted an extra horn I'd just play. I had plenty of bread so I wasn't worried about money.

Chicago: Was this a happy period for you?

Lester: Oh yeah, I've always been happy. I been happy all my life.

Chicago: You felt good about the music and the way you were growing; the transitions and changes.

Lester: Yeah, shit yeah, I was happy. I had a '51 classic Bentley, a motorcycle, a hip apartment in Chicago, I was plenty happy.

Chicago: When did you hook-up with the AACM (Association for the Advancement of Creative Musicians) cats?

Lester: Well, when I first came to Chicago I was doing a lot of sessions down at Chess Records. You know, jingles and other stuff. There were cats down there that later went on to become Earth Wind and Fire. In fact Maurice White was the studio drummer; a lot of cats were around in there then. But I was bored. So they had this cat to take me around. One day he asked if I wanted to go to a AACM rehearsal; he said I wouldn't be bored. So, Muhal Richard Abrams was having the rehearsal, man, I had never seen so many weird motherfuckers in my life . . . in one place. I said this is home here. As a musician there's always a couple of dudes you hang with. But here was thirty or forty crazy motherfuckers all in one spot. I mean Roscoe Mitchell, Anthony Braxton, and Abrams; eccentric type cats. So I made that rehearsal and Muhal had me play a solo. Before I got home good the phone was ringing. Cats calling up asking me to be in their band. Roscoe Mitchell, I hooked-up with him. He had his own band, The Roscoe Mitchell Quartet. So this was fun and it was a challenge. And I always wanted to be a Jazz musician. I was doing pretty good with what I was doing. So, I didn't really need the bread; I could do what I wanted to do. You know, my old lady had a hit record out and I was working. Shit, I was paying myself a salary. So, when I got into the AACM it was a real challenge. I always wanted to be more than just a studio musician. I wanted to be like Miles and Dizz and those cats. . . a professional Jazz Musician.

Chicago: When was the transition made to the Art Ensemble of Chicago?
Lester: Well, Roscoe aleady had a group that featured me. The Roscoe Mitchell Quartet; featuring Lester Bowie. Then we decided to have equal contribution without featuring anybody's name. So we called ourselves the Art Ensemble. It wasn't until 1969 when we went to France that we became the Art Ensemble of Chicago. The French gave us that name I guess to differentiate us from other musicians. Then the name stuck.

Chicago: Was there any particular reason all of you decided to get up and go to France.
Lester: Yes. We wanted to be professional musicians playing Jazz. Up until this point I was a professional playing different types of gigs. One day over at Chess records or with Fontella, the next day with the Art Ensemble or Jackie Wilson. We found that we had a unique style—a unique way of playing together, and we wanted to do that exclusively for our whole living. We felt the only way we could do that would be to pack up as a unit and start developing our concepts together, somewhere else. Since some people had expressed interest in us in France, and we had records out over there, and they were pretty popular, France was the natural choice. It turned out to be a good move. I sold all of my furniture and everything to help finance the move. We moved over with money 'cause I had a lot of shit. We wasn't on no street corners, we had a beautiful crib in Sainte Leu la Forêt.

Chicago: Tell me about your arrival, the landing. That must have really been something.
Lester: Oh, man. We came into France with a Volkswagen van full of instruments, and I had two kids with me at that time.

Chicago: Did you come on a ship?
Lester: Yeah. Music life is a great time if you just go on and trust it. Yeah we came on a ship. The captain found out we were musicians and gave us a place to practice. I mean this trip was a gas. New York to Le Havre. This was the last sailing to the United States. And the staff was all Brothers; the kitchen, waiters, everybody. We hung with the crew, and we was probably the only Blacks on as passengers.

Chicago: Did you finance most of the trip?
Lester: Yeah, but that then didn't bother me. It wasn't like taking a chance or anything. Anytime you take a band intact anywhere you're going to work. You can take an intact band to the Jungle or Siberia. They're gone say, 'Give them a gig.' A Black band especially—anywhere in the world you can work. We were working within three days of hitting France. We were working three nights a week.

Chicago: How long did it take you to find a place to live?
Lester: We stayed in a hotel about three days. Then we found a real estate agent, dropped a couple of thousand dollar bills on him, and boom, we was in business.

'Yes monsieur, whatever you want.' We got that big house in St. Leu.

Chicago: When I arrived in France at age twenty I was wild eyed and eager to swallow up as many new adventures and experiences as possible. I— my partner and I—added a couple of new definitions to words like wild, fun, and lustful. How did yal feel just being there?

Lester: You always feel good finally doing what you want to do. We were finally playing the music that we like to play. We were having a ball, I mean we were having a ball—the cats were going crazy. Plus Paris was jumping then too. The revolutionary thing was happening; political multiculturalism was happening. Then there's just the idea that we were over there making it. We supported our families, we had a nice house. We went over there with one truck and came back with four trucks. So without specific details of everything that happened—it was a great time. But we gradually got tired of it. We wanted to go home eventually.

Chicago: How long were you there?
Lester: Two years.

Chicago: Through the vine, I heard yal was having a rough time with the French at one time.
Lester: Oh yeah. One time the tax man confiscated all of our shit: trucks, instruments, everything. Then they had us in jail. But we got that rectified pretty quickly. Then we got kicked out of France once.

Here's what happened: There was a radio program about us on Radio Luxembourg; it was just about us. The show portrayed us as revolutionaries, damn-near Black Panthers, and by the way, they happen to live in St. Leu la Foret. So the big boys in St. Leu were like 'What, they live here?' So the order to oust us came not from the police, but from way up, some royalty. A lot of the land in France is still owned by royal families that have some clout. You know, dukes and duchesses. In reality the other people come up under them, the mayors and police chiefs.

So this thing was like a movie. The next day after the broadcast the police showed up at our door. Some inspector in a trench coat with a grimace on his face. He had two uniformed cats with him as back-ups. So our dogs had them stopped at the gate (that's from our military training). They told us if we didn't leave town they would escort us to the border. Well we were planning to hit the road the next day anyway, so their threat didn't make a difference.

Chicago: Hit the road like Gypsies?
Lester: Yeah, we were Gypsies all that summer. We had all the equipment: trucks, tents, stoves, heaters, everything. I had my family. We had police dogs. I tell you, we were ready. We stayed at campsites all over.

Chicago: Did yal have some gigs lined up?
Lester: Yeah, some, but we were out there on the road. Gypsies. You see there are so many things you can do collectively. I mean we were living

good out there. A couple of grand from a gig would go a long way. We lived in camps for the entire summer of 1970. We ended up in Sweden, then we moved on into hotels when it got too cold.

Chicago: So you must have had a good scouting thing happening?
Lester: Oh yeah. And the military training thing was key. Advance scouts would check out all kind of shit: gigs, food, people, etc. But like I said, if you got a band intact, you gone get some gigs. How you gone be a Black band, and ain't gone get no gigs? Who in the world don't wanna hear no Black folks play no music? I don't understand why cats get scared to go on out there.

Chicago: That's how I've always felt. Just go on out there . . . even just me and the harp. So, having lived and played in France, what are your impressions of the French people?
Lester: Well they're kind of doggish—not all of them, quite a few have personalities. I mean most Europeans' background is one of wars and colonization of Africa. I mean really, they've dogged a lot of people. And they have this kind of presumed intelligence, they presume that they're really cultured. And they are in a certain sense, but in other ways they're really barbaric, crude. Most western nations are like that. They didn't get to be big western nations walking on roses or no shit like that. I mean they became France by cutting off motherfuckers' heads.

Chicago: So, after the Gypsy adventures were you stateside bound?
Lester: Yeah, we headed back on a boat, an Italian boat. I believe it was the Michaelangelo. With all the equipment and stuff that was the only way we could travel. And I tell you we had some great voyages on boats.

Chicago: Still at the time of your return the Art Ensemble did not have a name in the States. What was your game plan for developing your market and keeping the music together?
Lester: Once we left Europe we knew we could always work there. That's the way we set it up. We wanted to go back to the States because we wanted to be home. If we couldn't get no work, that didn't matter because we would be home. But we knew we could work in Czechoslovakia, or Warsaw or somewhere. We had set up a network. See, we approached this as world marketing for our music, not on just a local or national level, but worldwide. If you got your thing going internationally, you gone work. You may have to go far, but you work. We have to go to Tokyo next week. We can't buy a gig in Chicago, but we have to go to Tokyo. So we set that up years ago. I just can't imagine living in those places though. After a while it wears on you. Different country, different land. You have to talk slow to be understood. I mean if you want to assimilate into their thing, like becoming French, that's another thing. To me it ain't no gas to be French. I like being an American Negro. I like that.

Chicago: You like being a blood?
Lester: I like it.

Chicago: You've played a lot of music with countless groups and your own groups: Brass Fantasy, Roots to the Source, and others. Who would you like to be musically.
Lester: I would like to be America's favorite trumpet player. Lester Bowie, a household word.

Chicago: You've had all kinds of times with money . . . lots of money, little money. What do you think of money?
Lester: I like cash. It's not an end. It's like a tip, a little extra. Like I say though, I have had fun. I can't remember a time when I was truly depressed. Money does not determine my success, although money is nice to have. I mean I bought a Lexus, being me. I would never change who I am though to have some money. If I can't afford something I want, I'll just wait until I can.

Chicago: So you're not thrifty or conservative with money.
Lester: No. I'm a spendthrift actually. I waste a lot of money by normal standards. I could try to put the brakes on it but I don't think of it as such. I spend a lot of money. I tip heavy, cause I know people that wait tables is working hard too. Plus them heavy tips get you good service.

Chicago: Has your life been gratifying?
Lester: Yeah, and that's the amazing thing. I'm a family man. You can manage all these things and still be a responsible citizen. The biggest and best thing I got going is my family.

Chicago: Want another cognac?
Lester: Yeah.

Chicago: Would you make a final comment on the state of financial affairs of Blues and Jazz?
Lester: I think some white performers ought to start paying royalties to Negroes. I think the motherfucking Rolling Stones ought to build a six block recreational, cultural facility for Black folks on the Westside; where they made their money from. I think all these white entertainers that have used Black music should pay some sort of royalties. The Rolling Stones need to go down to them joints with a basket of money, and pass out a few million dollars. If they were really righteous that's what I believe they would do. They've stolen a lot of music, but I don't want to just fault white people; I have to fault Black people too. I mean, we just gave our shit away. I know what they've done . . . but we're stupid enough to let motherfuckers have the shit, in a sense you can't blame someone for using it.

Chicago: Lester, we have to continue this conversation soon. Thanks.
Lester: Anytime, anywhere in the world . . . thank you.

LESTER BOWIE CONTINUED

July 1, 1997, Bologna

Chicago: What did you and the Art Ensemble cats envision when the decision was made to go to Paris?
Lester: I already knew what was going to be happening. I mean I didn't go to Paris and put up all this cash unless I knew what was going to be happening. I thought the shit through thoroughly beforehand. First of all I knew that we had something when we all met under whatever circumstances. And we are entirely different, every last one of us, and we have different interpretations as to how and why we were formed. But whatever the reasons were, once we had formed, I saw then that this could be a lasting entity. Once I saw that I started thinking of ways to move us ahead. I had been a pro in music for a long time when I met the Art Ensemble cats. It was like we were not youngsters, 17 or 18; cats were grown. I had been on the road since the 50s. So, I knew exactly what we were doing. I knew we had something different and unique, not only in terms of music, but in terms of a vision. And I felt at that time that this was something that could last quite awhile; and it has lasted. Once that thought was completely clear, I said, alright, let's sell all the furniture and move to France. We had to start making a living doing what we were doing. We had to focus on this sort of music, this sort of ensemble, to advance to the next level.

Chicago: You had a completely clear and confident vision?
Lester: Yes. It had to be strong. You ain't going to commit your wife and sell all the furniture if it ain't damn strong.

Chicago: Now all of you were grown. Been in the military, some of you had families and other responsibilities. So you were professionals with a collective music vision going on an adventure to further all the aspects. Right? Tell me.
Lester: The thing we were trying to figure out was how we were going to survive playing this music which was so different from anything else. To figure out a way to survive doing what we liked was the issue; and I've always been good at that sort of thing. Since I saw that we was a happening thing, then it was just a matter of logistics. We had to go where the music was being listened to. It was not being listened to everywhere. In Paris it was being listened to. So, let's go to Paris.

   Part of the job of a musician is that of a messenger. If you ain't ready to be a messenger, forget it. You need to get a job in the post office or somewhere. If you ain't ready to travel, pack up your family, or pack up yourself and hit the road, you're in the wrong business. Because that's what music is about. It's about spreading knowledge and education, and re-education. It's about spreading. You have got to travel with it to spread the word. Like all the people in the past that have had to travel to spread the music. We knew that, and we knew we had something unique to deal with. It was just a matter of logistics. There wasn't no profound vision like Christ coming off a mountain and saying, 'Go forth to Paris.' It was like, they are listening in Paris. So we were trying to make a living. We wanted to do what we were doing, and also maintain our families. We wanted to maintain doing something we really believed in. At the time Roscoe was working another job making calculators or something. Malachi was in a Holiday Inn piano bar type situation. I was with Jackie Wilson one day, Jerry Butler the next; you know, that whole scene.

So we said we want to make something out of this thing we had going on. And to do that we had to first of all pack up and go some place where people would listen. And that place was Paris.

Chicago: In terms of the exploration of sound. The Art Ensemble has cats playing all types of instruments as well as gongs, tings, pings, whistles, blocks, bells and shouts; you name it. What's the motivation behind the sound searching?

Lester: The motivation is that we are free to do whatever we feel like doing. The motivation is to extend your imagination to put what you imagine into practice. It might not work. Everything I play don't work. Every concert we play has not been successful in terms of doing what we wanted to do. But we tried to do something. We always have the impetus to *try* and do something different. How could we survive doing something different? Doing something people aren't familiar with. How to make this music acceptable. That was the challenge. A lot of times you have to play a normal note for someone to listen to an abnormal note. Once they hear you play a normal one, they say, 'Ok' and then they'll listen. If you start off with an abnormal note they'll never listen at all. It's finding a balance to get the people to hear what we are hearing. I don't really put the emphasis on the music so much. We had the music. Once we all met we knew we had something. We knew our thing could work. The trick was to make this work, because at the same time we got kids and grand kids. The emphasis was on making it work. That's why we had to move. We couldn't make a living in Chicago. As long as we was in Chicago, Roscoe had to work his straight gig, I had to keep with Jackie Wilson or whoever. But in France we could be the Art Ensemble. That's the reason we went to France.

Chicago: And the visuals. How did the visuals come about?

Lester: The visuals came about about because we have an unlimited imagination. Whoever had an idea or whatever combination of ideas, we tried them. If we wanted to run out in the audience we did it. We didn't have any mental encumbrance on what we wanted to do. We weren't restricted to bebop, free jazz, dixieland, theater, or poetry. We could put it all together. We could sequence it any way we felt like it. It was entirely up to us. We didn't have any preset standards. We were open to try anything. Everything didn't work, but we were free to try it.

Chicago: As time moved on, have things piqued, are they still moving, and where?

Lester: Everything that we had thought and projected started happening in Paris. In Paris we really practiced what we preached. That was the first time we actually were the Art Ensemble; and functioning as such, that music was our life blood. At the same time we haven't done everything that we want to do. Our vision has never dimmed. There have been certain limitations in terms of how much of what we were doing has been accepted. You have to find a balance: how much is going to be accepted, how to keep food on the table. Fortunately, we have been able to do our own thing and keep food on the table. We have been able to survive as a unit playing what we want to play. There are many things we want to do that we have not yet done; and there are many things we visualize we have not gotten to yet. We did learn how to survive as the Art Ensemble playing the music that we play.

Chicago: Has the Art Ensemble moved any nearer into the listening range of the American public?

Lester: I don't think we've moved into anything significant in America yet. We're not really listened to in America. I mean they had a festival in New York honoring Louis Armstrong; they had every trumpet player in town there but me. The Art Ensemble doesn't work that much in the States. We have just a few listeners. The thing is we realized that we had to do our thing with a planetary approach. We had to hit the world market. We couldn't localize. It just could not be Chicago or New York. *The only way for us to survive was to develop a world audience. World music, the whole world concept.* In fact that whole World Music thing they doing now comes from the Art Ensemble. We were the first ones to start bringing in African and Indian influences and making them meaningful with what we were doing. But once again in terms of America, I don't ever feel as though we have been accepted. I feel like an outlaw when it comes to the States. I feel like an old outlaw now. It's like the James' Gang.

Chicago: When you do play in America, it must be a unique and loyal audience that comes and listens. I saw you at the Beverly Hills Theater in Beverly Hills, California of all places, and the house was packed. Who are these people?

Lester: By approaching our business on a world level, we always have a full house. People will come from everywhere to see us play. Though our performances are rare in the States, there is a certain element of people who want to hear us, or who have been following us for years. The people at the Beverly Hills concert may have seen us the last time in Germany, France, or Japan. That's the benefit of world marketing. In fact every concert we play is sold out no matter were it is. It could be Istanbul or Los Angeles. We have developed an audience world-wide, regardless if we have been accepted by the industry or the media. And that's what we went for from the beginning; to develop a real audience. That's who we really play for now. We don't give a fuck about the record companies. We don't give a fuck about the media. We don't give a fuck about none of them. We don't bear any animosity toward the industry, they don't really come into play. I

Lesters Bowie's Brass Fantasy, 1985

Left to right: B. Stewart, S. Torre, P. Wilson, F. Lacy, L. Bowie, S. Davis, V. Chancey, M. Thompson, R. Saddik

don't give a fuck what they do, because they don't effect my existence or my family's. My family depends upon what I do, and what we do as a unit as the Art Ensemble. What people have to understand is that in this business a lot has to do with luck. A lot has to do with direction and vision. You don't get the luck until you are headed the right way. You don't get blessed if you are doing the wrong shit. We've been very lucky. Things have happened and we've done some great gigs. We have met some great people. Things have happened because we have maintained who we are. We are not trying to be the media darlings, we are not trying to be mainstream. We are not only entertainment, we are education, refinement, culture. We are the Art Ensemble, not a Jazz Ensemble. We are playing music intended to elevate your intellect. We want people to think. We want people to say, 'What the fuck was that? Why did they do that? How does that relate to that Blues piece they were playing?' We are into being accepted. It's not that we don't want to be accepted, but we have to be accepted for who we are.

Chicago: What's the game-plan for this new era. By that I mean communications like the Internet and the new technology?

Lester: We have been anticipating the Internet for years. We play for the people who have supported us throughout the years. That's what we are concerned about. The people in Italy, France, America, everywhere where they have supported us. We are actually playing for them rather than breaking new ground anymore, or attracting new listeners, even though of course, we always do. We're at the end of our careers. We are close to 60 years old, with one of us already 70. We are not going to be active that much longer. We're trying to round out what we're doing. What we are doing now is for the people that supported us all this time. We are going to make everything available to the people who have supported us: books, records, videos; all will be available on the Internet and various other means. Now we're working for them. We have done our major work as far as trying to reach out. And we are really thankful to the people who have helped us survive. We are really thankful to our fans. They have really enabled us to be as weird as we are. To be able to be citizens, to have families. I am really thankful to the people of France, Africa, America, Japan, all over the world, who have enabled me to survive long enough to raise my family.

We getting ready to get down now so heavy in the music that nobody would dare publish it but us. We have the means now because of the work and the people over the years. All will be available on the Internet. Live performances will be somewhat limited, because like I said we are close to 60; and we been out here fighting. We still fighting—like for 32 years. We never did have an easy break. It wasn't as if we had a group together for 10 years, and the next thing it was cool. We still struggling. But like I said, live performances will be limited as we move nearer the year 2000. I'm retiring; October 11, 2001 I'm outta here. I been working hard all my life. I got a bottle of wine I bought 15 years ago that won't even be ready until 2001. I'm opening it October 11, 2001.

'We're interested in the totality of the musical expression in every way.
We deal with visuals as an enhancement of the music.
The tradition of Black musical expression has always been more than
just playing an instrument. It's always involved elements of showmanship.
You can go back to minstrel shows, and vaudeville, and beyond that to
earlier times. People came to see a person get up there and deal:
dancing, singing, a total creative expression.
We try to recapture that spirit in our music.
We deal with certain kinds of symbolism that have their roots in
African tradition - West African, mainly. The idea of the face paint is taking
our personal being that we bring to the concert, trying to leave that outside
of the music and evolving ourselves up to a higher level on stage.
Part of the ritual of face painting is to evoke the spirits, and to do that
you have to transform your earthbound appearance.
Involved in that also is the color concept.
The different
combinations of color evoke
different kinds of responses and set up different kinds of vibrations.
This is a way of projecting an idea, a feeling, a certain mood.
Different patterns make different symbolisms.
They might not mean anything to the people who see them,
but that's only because they don't understand the symbols.
But if the symbols are presented correctly they still have an effect
whether you understand them or not.'

Famoudou Don Moye

FAMOUDOU DON MOYE INTERVIEW - PART 1

Lincoln T. Beauchamp, Jr
'Chicago Beau'

My friendship with Famoudou Don Moye is entering its third decade. It has been one of music, adventure and rich experiences. Many dreams have been realized; much music has been played. The following interview takes a look at the life, thoughts and musical philosophy of one of the world's foremost percussionist.

August 1988

Chicago Beau: Your career is entering the third decade. You play with *The Art Ensemble of Chicago*, Lester Bowie's *Brass Fantasy*, *The Leaders*; and as a soloist, and band leader. You are on the move constantly playing around the globe. You are considered by many, including myself, to be one of the most progressive percussionists in the world. You have won the Downbeat Poll six out of the last eight years. You are a force in world music—Black music; tell me something of the beginning of Don Moye, the musician.

Famoudou Don Moye: My father was a drummer. I have four uncles that were playing in bands in the 40s. My grandmother was a member of the *Daughters of the Eastern Star* which was a women's auxiliary equivalent of the *Benevolent Paternal Order of the Elks*; she was involved in the leadership. They had concerts and everything in the 30s, 40s, and 50s. They brought in Duke Ellington and other big bands of the times, she would often talk about the music and the times they had at their annual conventions. My father and his sisters and brothers were also members of the Elks which had a big band, and a marching band and drum majorettes and all of that. They also had a couple of jazz combos.

So, all this was prior to my being around jazz per se. My grandmother was a cook and a caterer. She had her own restaurant for awhile. She did all the food service for the Elks Hall, which was right next door to her house. She lived upstairs over a club called the Pythod. I used to stay there with her often. The club brought in people like Johnny Lytell, Grant Green, Brother Jack McDuff, Jimmy McGriff, and Kenny Burrell, and Rhythm and Blues, and Blues. I met a lot of the cats playing there when they came by to eat. I was in a drum and bugle corps, and singing in the church choirs. My mother used to always take us out to see opera and concerts; she took us to a lot of different musical situations. I can remember going to see operas in the summer at open-air concerts in the park. We might see the opera one week and then the next week we'd go see the Mormon Tabernacle Choir. And then the next week Mahalia Jackson. There was always something. She took us out to a big variety of musical events, dance and theater. Sometimes she would get tickets for the big shows at the Eastman Theater.

Chicago: As a child listener, you were never under-exposed to varied musical forms.
Moye: Never. I was always listening, studying, and checking things out. I was fascinated and in awe of the musicians I met at my grandmother's place. And then records, we had all kind of records. My mother likes classical music a lot. And I had a cousin that played vibraphones, tenor sax, and drums. He had a lot of jazz, Rhythm and Blues records, a lot of Fats Domino and Ray Charles. We had all the Black popular music of the time; James Brown, B. B. King, everybody. There was a pretty wide variety of music. I was also into Gospel music. My barber was in the sanctified church and they played

all the great Gospel tunes in his shop all of the time.

Chicago: As you were coming up, there was music all around, all the time!
Moye: Yep, umm-hm. For a small town that scene was cool.

Chicago: When did you take the big plunge and decide, 'Hey, I want to do this for a living,' 'I want this to be my life'?
Moye: Hm. That kind of happened gradually. There never was a moment that all of a sudden, wake up, 'I'm gonna do this!' I was going to college, doing gigs around, and then a chance came up.

Chicago: Where were you at this time?
Moye: I went to Central State University in Ohio, for a couple years, then I transferred to Wayne State University in Detroit for a specific purpose; to be in an urban environment and for the musical exposure. I was gigging around, checking all the sessions and subbing for different cats, when the drummer from one of the bands I was playing congas with took a gig with a rock band. I took his place, and soon we came up with a scheme to go to Europe. I thought this was an okay deal. We named ourselves Detroit Free Jazz. The personnel in the band was Ron Mikller, bass; Art Fletcher, sax and percussion; Tom Powell, percussion; Bob Sklar, piano.

I left school and went on the road in the USA, and shortly, on to Europe, where things evolved very well. We traveled all over in our own truck with an upright piano, bass, drums, and everything we needed. The band broke up after fourteen months. I maintained by doing lots of side gigs and working with dance companies playing percussion for classes and performances. I **worked and lived all over: Morocco, Paris, Rome, Vienna, Copenhagen, Lausanne, Munich, Amsterdam, and Milano.**

Chicago: I imagine you had many adventures in those places.
Moye: Oh yeah, yeah, yeah. You know Beau, you've been around, there's never a conscious question of 'what am I doing with my life?' Things kind of evolve naturally if you let them. There was never a moment that I had to sit down and say, "O.K., what am I gonna do with my life?' and all that. It never was even an issue. It never has been. I just kept doing what I was doing. There were times when— not so much 'what am I gonna do with my life?,' but 'what am I gonna do about my next meal?'

Chicago: What am I gonna do about this flop?
Moye: Not really. I always had a decent place to stay. I didn't have that much money, but every time I got paid, I would spend my money on instruments.

Chicago: For you, are 'survival' and 'music' synonymous?
Moye: They sure are.

Chicago: I understand you spent some time in North Africa. How was that?
Moye: It was great. I just dove into that scene. I was hanging out and playing with the Ganouahs in Essaouira, and Marrakech, Morocco. I also spent a lot of time in Tangiers. That's where I first met Randy Weston. He had a big club there, and was very well connected.

Chicago: Where are the Ganouahs from?
Moye: As far as I know, they are all over the country, but come mainly from the south. They were concentrated in the bigger cities, especially Marrakech. I used to play with them daily, practicing and learning the rhythms, and their grooves. They had many unique instruments. Many different types of drums, flutes, and strings. The music would go on and on into a trance-

like state, accompanied by surreal dancing and chanting.

Chicago: On my first visit to Senegal I noticed a similarity in some of the musical styles—similar to Blues and bebop. Was music in Black Africa a revelation to you?

Moye: Well, of course. But, I had already met up with a lot of African cats in the States and in Paris. Detroit was a good experience for me, because I met a lot of musicians from Nigeria, Ghana, and East Africa. When I was learning congas they showed me a lot of the styles and rhythms and everything. So, I started working with different African groups, sometimes with as many as 15 people in the group. We would perform with dancers, singers, and full ensembles.

I had a similar experience in Paris. I was playing and studying with a Master Drummer from the Congo named Titos Sompa. And there were other drummers around from Mali, Ivory Coast, Guinea, and Senegal. I also worked with Kenyan dancer, Elsa Wolliaston.

I got into the languages; Wolof and Bambara. I didn't learn a lot of grammar but I got familiar with their structures, sounds, slang and colloquialisms. Music lives in the language, language lives in the music. By the time I got to Africa, I was updating and expanding my information.

Chicago: When did you first go to Sub-Saharan Black Africa?

Moye: The first time, 1985. When I got there I was well prepared, and the feeling was very natural. It was really a matter of remembering my international rules of travel: cash, equipment, return ticket, and always find the musicians and creative people first, leave the tourist shit alone, and good things will happen.

I got married to my wife, Gloria, in Freetown, Sierra Leone, West Africa. The legal ceremony was performed at the American Embassy by Ambassador Arthur Lewis, a Jazz fan who bore a striking resemblance to Dizzy Gillespie. One of the best men was Christian Nakonz, the German Ambassador. The ceremony was under the auspices of the Minister of Justice. The traditional wedding party was held at the Sierra Leone Cultural Village, where dancers and drummers from the tribes performed for us for a couple of days.

Chicago: Did you have similar experiences in other parts of the Black World?

Moye: The same thing happened in Haiti, Guadeloupe, and Jamaica. I had already done my research prior to going to these countries, and I spoke passable French. In Guadeloupe, I knew many musicians, because while I was touring in France, I met a group called the Caribbe Jazz Ensemble from Guadeloupe. Over the course of four or five years and several tours, we performed together at major festivals: Nice, Nancy, and Paris. When I got to Guadeloupe, we had great musical collaborations, and contacts for everything I needed. In Haiti there were musicians there I had known in New York and Paris. When I got there the music was happening. I didn't have to find the music, it was happening everywhere.

Chicago: Throughout the Black Diaspora; South America, North America, the Caribbean, and parts of Europe, it seems like Africa has influenced the music of the world more than any other kind of music.

Moye: Yeah, it's the strongest force on the planet, musically. It has contributed the most. African music is expressed through Black American's creativity. Black American music is the only music that you can go anywhere in the world and hear it. I've heard Duke Ellington's music all over the world, in every country I've ever been in. Pure. I've heard some form of Black music as part of the street sounds that you hear in any place you go. And that's the only kind of music that I've ever had that experience with.

Chicago: How would you define Blues?
Moye: Hm. It's a true derivative of our African tradition of music—the rhythmic part, the vocalization, chord structures and everything. So—I mean—real Blues is the direct channel to the ancient music.

Chicago: Like field hollers?
Moye: Yeah, it goes all the way back to griots. It's a direct link to the griots and our heritage. If it's got Blues in it, that's the unifying form.

Chicago: It's the undisputed link!
Moye: That's right as far as I'm concerned. I hear that in all the Black folk forms; I hear that same element. There's a unifying element that you don't hear in other music. Jazz is a derivative form; and Rhythm and Blues is a derivative form, and real Blues is the pure strain. Even if it's modern and extensive, it's remained closer to the original source. All of the music has expanded because of the wealth of information. We're living in a time of maximum exposure to a lot of bullshit. Of all of these derivatives, real Blues has remained closest to true form.

Chicago: Historically Blues artists have paid mega-dues. Unfortunately, there has been little unity among the artists in so far as the business aspect of the music goes. But many Blues themes represent a defiance—defiance of social norms and of religious ones among many. But rarely is there a defiance of the white controlled music business. In the music, you seldom detect dissent which I think is vital to Blues People, being in control of all aspects of their art. What are your thoughts on that?
Moye: Defiance is just one level of it. Along with defiance you have organization. There have been moments of defiance throughout the history of the music, but the strength of the effort and the strength of the cooperation between the musicians and their unity of effort is what enables us to survive. Any time the musicians are not strong in their unity, the control factor goes over to the *other* side.

Chicago: I know you and your people are dedicated to carrying the torch.
Moye: Well, we're doing our part. We're using our organization. We've got people doing writing, music publishing, arranging and composing, archival work, and other pursuits. We've got our video people, we're recording, producing, and performing. We're not solely interested in expanding our staff, we're interested in increasing the impact of what we are doing and having our staff and efforts be more effective.

Chicago: I think you all are going to have a serious impact on the world, man, a serious impact.
Moye: You've got that right. I just finished a tour with Brass Fantasy. In addition to performing, I'm road manager. Most of the business on the road goes through me; I'm the man that gets the money and does logistics. That's one less thing that Lester Bowie has to worry about. It's a demanding job. I'm utilizing our network. I do the road managing for the Leaders and the Art Ensemble, too; it's logical; let's expand the business potential for all the groups at the same time. It works out well, and it gives me a low tolerance for bullshit from agents, and producers, because we are trying to do this whole thing as professionally as possible.

Chicago: Entrepreneurs!
Moye: Yes, and more.

Chicago: Bluesmen and twentieth-century griots?
Moye: That's right, that's it. Urban Bushmen!

Chicago: Urban Bushmen. I hear you. Ancient to the Future!

Art Ensemble Of Chicago
30 Year Anniversary Tour
A Salute To The Afrikan Drum

Top row: Driver, Silah Allen, Enoch Williamson, Bahnamous Bowie, Christof Hetzel
Middle row: DonAlonzo Beauchamp, Mamane Samake, Babu Atiba, Meshach Silas,
Front row: Malachi Favors Maghostut, Larry Stevenson, Famoudou Don Moye, Roscoe Mitchel, Deborah Bowie, Lester Bowie.

FAMOUDOU DON MOYE CONTINUED

September 17, 1997, Bologna

Chicago Beau: Moye, how long had you been aware of the Art Ensemble before you became a member?
Famoudou Don Moye: Five years.

Chicago: And where was that awareness from?
Moye: Detroit. I was going to school there [Detroit], and they used to rehearse near the campus of Wayne State at a place called the Artists Workshop; a cooperative of artists, painters, poets, writers, dancers, and musicians, that was put together by John Sinclair. That's where I first met and studied with trumpeter, Charles Moore, who told me to go and check out the band. That was my first Art Ensemble concert.

Also during that time I was an editor for some of the publications printed by the Artists Workshop. That's where I first got into publishing and the kind of thing you're into, Beau.

Chicago: So who was the nucleus?
Moye: Lester, Roscoe, Malachi, and sometimes Philip Wilson. I saw them in Detroit on several occasions, that's how I got hooked on the dream of playing with them.

Chicago: And Joseph?
Moye: He had his own band. I saw them in Detroit too.

Chicago: When you met up with the cats in Paris, what particular things about them struck you for you to want to be a part of them?
Moye: They was WERKIN all the time. Cats was WERKIN! In the essence of the particularization of wanting to work with them, that was pretty much formed when I had seen them in Detroit. The open ended creative aspect of what they were trying to do is what hooked me. I knew they were looking for a drummer, and I knew that they was WERKIN all the time. They had trucks and a big crib out in the country. Everybody that was in Paris knew about that scene. Cats had motorcycles and all kinds of shit. That was a successful band doing their own thing, you know.

Chicago: Did you imagine that the organization would stay intact this long?
Moye: I pretty much figured it would. When you are doing it every day you don't really think of an end, you just think about what's going to be happening until the next payday, or the next project. With some groups there is always a limit; an externally imposed limitation usually coming from cats' unwillingness to take care of business. We didn't have that limitation. So there was no reason to have doubts as to our longevity. We were focused on the next scheme or angle we could come up with to do what we wanted to do. It was never predicated on work per se, it was predicated on doing what we want to do, and the timeliness of when we

felt things could reasonably be accomplished, not on anybody else's terms but ours. There was never any reason to see an ending, only continuation of the activities to the next project, or the completion of projects already in motion.

Chicago: There are a couple of versions regarding your hook-up with the Art Ensemble, can you clarify what you recall?
Moye: I was in Rome working with Steve Lacy in '69, then I moved to Paris. I was working with a lot of people in Paris, and Steve Lacy's band also. The Art Ensemble was looking for a drummer. They were playing at the American Center one night, and I used to keep all of my instruments there. They were up there playing; I just set up my stuff and started playing with them. They had seen me playing with Steve Lacy anyway, so somebody in the group, I don't know who, said they wanted to check out my stuff; my name had came up. After that they hired me. The first gig I did with them was for the film, *Les Stances à Sophie*. This was January or February 1970.

Chicago: Things were rolling pretty good for the band?
Moye: Yeah. From when I joined the band we did about five records right quick; and they had done about ten records before that. We were ready to go back to the States back in '71, but that's when the French authorities fabricated some tax shit, but all of our papers were in order. The French had confiscated all our instruments and put them in storage, but had to release our shit back because like I said, all of our shit was in order. In the process it occurred to us to let France go for awhile. We were ready to go back. We had the money to go back. The fine, five or ten grand, or whatever it was, cut in to our shit. We had to stay in Europe some more months to build our stash back up to get back. The fine ate up the money we had budget ed for the trans-Atlantic transportation, the boat and everything. I mean we had three trucks, personal stuff, equipment, and children. So we finally went back on the SS Rafaello out of Genova. That's when I first met Kunle Mwanga, then known as George Conley. When we got off the boat at the docks in New York, he was there to meet us. He was our first and only African American manager. I learned a lot of tricks about the music business from him. He booked tours in the States and Europe, and traveled with us extensively for five or six years.

We drove on to Chicago, Lester and his family went on to St. Louis. Soon after, Roscoe and me moved with all our instruments down to St. Louis for the summer. We set up at BAG, the Black Artists Group, a musicians cooperative similar to the AACM. We rehearsed and played constantly with all the cats from BAG Oliver Lake, Joe Bowie, Ajule Menelek, Bakida Carrol, Floyd Leflore, Julius Hemphil, Bobo Shaw, Bensid Thigpen. It was a totally creative environment of musicians, dancers, actors, poets, and painters. That's also where I met painter Emilio Cruz, who later did a bunch of album covers for us. We used to have concerts called the Sunrise Series. We'd start one day at noon and play all the way through till the sun came up the next day with continuous music featuring all the different groups and combinations. I met a lot of cats Lester grew up with. I also met Senegalese master drummer Mori Thiam. I was studying djembe with him and that's when I got into the exchange of information concept. I was studying African tradition with him, and he was studying African American tradition with me.

Chicago: After you got back to the US, how long was it before you started your campaign?

Moye: Things were in evolution. The corporate concept, the office, the various companies. We joined ASCAP in '74 as composers and publishers, after having already belonged to the French Society, SACEM. That was our first charter as a publishing company. In 1975 the office came into being which was located in a building owned by the Musicians Union. It was really my apartment with the dining alcove turned into office space. Eventually I got another space for my personal quarters. The office came into existence, strictly as an office in 1976 after I moved out.

Evod Magek, pianist, band leader, and community activist was doing a lot of work for us in this period. He maintained our phone lines, picked up mail, and did general monitoring of our office when we were on the road. He was actually our first paid office staff, because prior to his being with us, we had to shut the operation down until we returned. In those days we were often away for two or three months at a time. Evod also maintained the up-keep of our bus when we were out of the country. He also made a couple of West Coast tours with us as driver and travel technician. In the past he had done the same for Eddie Harris, travelling all over the States.

John Jackson was my real mentor for running the office and taking control of AEC business. He was a professional administrator from the old school. Never late, never absent, no days off for 30 years. Straight ahead function. He started with us part time for a few years and then retired and came on full time. That was a period of real growth for us, and we got our first corporate charter in 1979. He got us together on banking, bookkeeping, and general office management, and eventually started booking gigs too. He was also an accomplished trumpet player, even though he didn't start playing seriously till he was almost 40 years old. He dedicated his life to his own principles and those of the AACM and ART ENSEMBLE. Jackson worked right up to the day he died. He came in that day, put in his hours, said he wasn't feeling well, went to the hospital, and was gone by 4:00a.m. the next morning. Dedicated to the very end.

Chicago: What was it like in this period, the 70s for the music, gigs?
Moye: There was definitely a lot of activity. I was involved in many personal projects in Chicago. I performed with Amina Meyers & Ajaramu, Threadgil, Kalaparusha, The Pharaohs (Sattisfield, Hippmo Don Myrick, Pete Cosey, Big Willie Wood), Darlene Blackburn Dancers, Von Freeman, Jimmy Ellis, Willie Pickens, Joel Brandon, Rahm Lee Davis, Val Gray Ward, Fred Anderson, Young John Young, Jesus Wayne, Atuque Harold Murray & the Sun Drummers, where I met most of the drummers and percussionists I still work with these days: Enoch Williamson, Selah Allen, Sura, Oye, Kewu, Shango Njoko, Meshach Silas, Atiba, Clifton Robinson, P.C. Cotton, and others. That whole scene was jumping hard everyday and I was hitting with at least six different groups plus AACM activities.

It was also in that period that I formed with Ari Brown and Luba Rashiek our original sextet.

The Art Ensemble played Madison, Wisconsin, and the Lenox Music Center in Massachusetts. The Ann Arbor Blues Festival was hip. I remember in '72 we did Live at Mandel Hall. That was January 15 and 16, 1972. I'll never forget those concerts. Great music. My first winter in Chicago—10 degrees, 2 feet of snow, blizzard conditions, and the place was packed: a live recording, standing room only! It was brutal outside, and that's when I decided to start spending my winters in California or NYC or some damn place else. We took most of that money when the deal went down through Bob Koester of Delmark Records, the same Bob Koester who did *As If It Were the Seasons* by Jarman and *Sound* by Roscoe Mitchell years before any other label was willing to take the risk. We took most of that cash and purchased a 1951 Greyhound bus. That was the latest vehicle purchase in a succession of previous vehicle purchases, including motorcycles and vans. With all our equipment, we had to have our own independent means of transportation!

Part of how we got through '73 was doing the recording sessions for Atlantic Records, *Baptizm* and *Fanfare for Warriors*. Mike Cuscuna was the producer of those sessions. Also in that period Lester did a couple of records; one called *Rope-a-Dope* when Muhammed Ali was doing the *Rope-a-Dope* on George Foreman. He had moved to New York, and I was in and out of New York during that period. Me and Jarman did several projects with Bob Cummins' India Navagation label. I also did dates with Don Pullen, Julius Hemphil, Hamiett Bluiet, Chico Freeman, and a lot of people on the New York scene. In that period people were calling Lester trying to do record deals with the AEC and his bands. ECM got in touch with Lester first because they were interested in Brass Fantasy.

Chicago: There was momentum moving out the 70's into the 80's.
Moye: Yeah, and we started going back to Europe. '77 was the first year that we went back to Europe. We had been there in '74, then we took a three year hiatus. After Montreux Festival in '74, and a lot of other festivals: Pori, Finland; Konigsberg, Norway; Pescara, Italy; there wasn't really much else happening. So rather than go back for less money than was acceptable, we said we ain't going back for awhile. We went to Japan for the first time in '74.

We traveled all over the States in our bus. That was another of our pioneering periods, when we'd put some cash together, hit the road, and rent a house-rehearsal space and play everyday for 8 to 10 hours consistently. We did that in Ann Arbor; San Jose, California; Eugene, Oregon; and we gigged all over the country, We did the Five Spot in NYC, and a lot of hits on the Loft Jazz Scene, especially Studio Rivbea and the Tin Palace. Also, DC. Space, Philadelphia; Atlanta and Athens, Georgia; Detroit, East Lansing, Austin, Houston, New Orleans, LA, San Diego, Vancouver, Seattle, Montreal, and Toronto. We really got into developing our own audience in the States. Any place where they were ready for the music, we took it directly to their door. It was also at that time that we put the same emphasis on development of our individual projects. The idea was to expand our ideas through our own personal bands, work on new music, and bring that back to the AEC context. It works even now because everyone always brings a new perspective to both situations.

Then in '77 the ECM deal came up. The ECM package, for whatever it was worth, included promotion, recording, touring, and tour support. When we went back in '77 we had an organized tour. That's when we had our first paid crew, and we took all of our instruments. In '74, Kunle Mwanga was going on tour with us, and we were working with a French agent named Michele Salut. We basically had been moving all of our equipment around ourselves; driving, setting up, playing the gig, breaking down, and driving on to the next hit. We had been doing that since I joined the band in '70. So that shit was starting to get old; we had too much equipment to move by ourselves AND do the gig too. '77 was when we hired our first roadie, an Austrian, Joe Harting, who we met through Thomas Stowsand and ECM. He died in 1985 on the Autobahn coming back from East Germany. He was in a wreck with Colin Walcot from Oregon who also died; fog on the highway. He was our first roadie, and he was a good friend. Shortly after that we started working with Ameen Muhammed, a talented trumpet player who went on to pursue his own career; Larry Stevenson, Enoch Williamson, drummer and percussionist; Rod Echols; Charles Arnold; David Holmes; Kudus Onisemoh; Pedro Banha; DonAlonzo Beauchamp; and others, who did their jobs and helped take our productivity to the next level. And especially Anne Pryor who has been our bookkeeper, office manager, and sometimes agent since 1987.

Inside of the hook with ECM and all of their press is when Outward Visions came into the picture. They were first called Rasa Artists; I had met them, Marty and Elaine Cann, in New York through Chico Freeman. They were the first American agents that actually committed to get together with us to combine our resources with their energy and willingness to deal. They came up with some nice projects. In 1980 we performed more than eighty concerts in the States. The Canns' timing was good because the ECM records were moving well. The entire collaboration lasted ten years. That was a highly productive period. We worked Toronto, Montreal, Miami, Knoxville, San Diego, Memphis, Cleveland, Detroit, Washington, Atlanta, Boston, Philadelphia, St. Louis, Beverly Hills, and a lot of hits in-between. I remember we ran into you and Earth, Wind, and Fire at the concert in Beverly Hills in '83. It was around the time we hooked up with Victor O'Gilvey. He didn't have nothing but talk about work in the States, but he had contacts in Europe and Japan. O'Gilvey hooked us up with Channel 4 in England who wanted to do a documentary on the Band. The result was The Great Black Music Video produced by Brian Izzard. O'Gilvey booked us in Japan in '84 where we hadn't been in ten years. He beat us out of $10,000—O'Gilvey and his people in Japan. What happened was we got our money, but we were going from Japan to Sicily. So we sent all of our instruments from Tokyo through Munich to Sicily by air cargo; O'Gilvey's boys didn't pay for the shipment up-front the way they were supposed to. They sent the shipment COD. We didn't find out until we got to Munich. So that was $10,000 we had to come up with on the spot in Munich for the airline to release the instruments and equipment. Fortunately, Thomas

Stowsand of ECM fronted us the cash to pay the cargo bill. And to top that off we had to spend an additional $3,000 for excess personal baggage at Tokyo airport.

We were working quite a bit in Europe again in this period, especially France, Belgium, Holland, and Scandinavia, with an agent named Philip deVisscher. He did quite a few AEC tours, and also put together a 10 concert project called The Sun Ra All-Stars with myself, Lester, Sun Ra (of course), Philly Joe Jones, Archie Shepp, Don Cherry, Richard Davis, John Gilmore, and Marshall Allen. We played the Berlin Jazz Festiva, l and the All-Stars flew to Brussels for a concert the next day, but Sun Ra had his whole Arkestra traveling by bus so he did the All-Stars concert, boarded his band bus for an 18 hour ride to Brussels, arrived, rehearsed with his band a couple of hours, then played the concert with us and played after that with the Arkestra and was ready to head for Paris for the All-Stars concert the next day at the Paris Jazz Festival.

The Leaders came into being during this period as a result of another one of Devisscher's all star band schemes. Me and Chico Freeman didn't want the concept to dissolve after only one tour. We wanted to develop a group and a concept with musicians that were interested in longevity and control of the music and the business: standard AEC & AACM principles adapted to a different group. That first Leaders line up was myself, Chico, Arthur Blythe, Cecil McBee, Don Cherry, and Hilton Ruiz. We really wanted Lester and Don Pullen, but Pullen was committed to his quartet with George Adams, and Lester said we weren't ready yet, and that was true. Plus, he was doing a lot of projects with Jack DeJohnette and also getting Brass Fantasy off to a solid start. Kirk Lightsey jumped on board next and we were rolling. Lester came in about '86 or so. I was also doing a lot of percussion work with Andrew Cyrille and we formed a group called, Pieces of Time, with Milford Graves and special guest artists: Kenny Clarke or Philly Joe Jones or Tani Tabbal. Sun Ra hit with us once too at Prospect Park in Brooklyn when Philly Joe was sick and couldn't make the gig.

Chicago: Did those Italian gigs involve Isio Saba?
Moye: Lester met Isio in '75. Isio did the first concert for us in Rome in '78 with an organization called Zigfield, that was headed by Fausta Gabrielle and Francesca Brazzi. The concert was part of an ECM tour.

Chicago: How long did the ECM thing last?
Moye: The last ECM record was called *Urban Bushman*. It was a double record recorded live at the America House in Munich. Then ECM became completely silent.

Chicago: When did DIW Records kick in?
Moye: They kicked in going into '87. We released a video to them and they bought the rights to AEC Live in Tokyo 1984. Those were our first projects with them. Prior to us, DIW was just doing re-issues. We were the first group that they actually contracted with to do new music in the studio. '88, '89 is when we first inked a ten-record deal. What we did with DIW is what

we do with everybody. We got a budget, produced it ourselves, then sent them the masters.

The DIW deal was fruitful because we further developed ourselves as producers and finally had a chance to do more of our special projects with our own groups as well as other artists. *The Art Ensemble of Chicago-Soweto* project was something we had conceived several years before. Lester and I were guest soloists in a concert at the Camden Jazz Festival in London. A project put together by one of the best production agencies for us in Europe, The Serious Productions Company headed by John Cummings and John Elway. They have always produced our projects in England at the highest conceivable artistic level. That concert at the Camden Fest was me and Lester featured in duo, and with the Amabutho Male Chorus from South Africa along with a dance company whose name I can't remember. We did the Paris Festival with that same group. Those initial concerts evolved into our AEC of Soweto project on DIW and another album called *America/South Africa US of A/U of SA*. We brought them to New York to record and did tours in Spain and Italy over the next couple of years. The last big project we did with them was for our 25th Anniversary tour with the AEC, Brass Fantasy, and Amabutho as a big band. Unfortunately, as usual, that was another project that never got done in the States. We also produced a CD for Joe Bowie's Defunkt and a special project with Cecil Taylor. Lester's New York Organ Ensemble with myself, Steve Turre, Kelvyn Bell, Amina Claudine Meyers, James Carter, and Philip Wilson also did two CDs. All in all we got a lot of mileage out of that deal, but DIW eventually became silent too. Shades of ECM I suppose. I remember calling you to see if you wanted to do a deal with them, on your terms of course. They created a whole separate Blues division through your input, and went ahead and further expanded their label. I hope yal got paid right and I'm glad you were able to seize that opportunity. Forward Motion!

Another fruitful collaboration was with Gabriele Kleinschmidt, GKP Promotions in Germany. She booked the Art Ensemble, The Leaders, Brass Fantasy, special projects: our 25th and 30th Anniversary Tours, the Deustche Kammerphilharmonie concerts, and the Brazzy Voices project with the Norwegian group, the Brass Brothers, as well as solo and guest appearances.

Chicago: Can you recall some Art Ensemble stories—adventures?
Moye: Oh yeah. We used to carry heat on the road. Jarman had his license as an international securities broker, he had a pearl handled .38 magnum. There was all kinds of crazy stuff going on back in the 70s. People were gettin jumped and shit; hijacked, and we were carrying cash. It was a whole thing we went through checking in, on and off the plane with the heat. We had our gun maintenance classes; the other cats were ex-servicemen anyway. When we used to travel in the States we had our licenses for our pieces. When we used to go out to the West Coast traveling cross country on our bus back in the 70s, you couldn't be too careful with them wild white people out there. We had shotguns and rifles. We've got film footage of rifle practice, and gun cleaning. We used to practice in the morning, then put the guns under the floorboard or up in the racks.

We were never messin with nobody. But people would come up on us all the time (five Black men in their own bus full of instruments and two dogs). I remember one time we going up to East Lansing, Michigan to get Roscoe, and the bus broke down in the middle of the night in the corn fields. Some of them roving vigilante types came up on the bus in their pick-ups, unmarked squad cars with lights flashing and shit. They had their rifles and guns out. They said, 'What you boys doin out here?' So we got back in the bus and came out with our guns and said, 'What YOU BOYS doing?' They said, 'Uh uh we was just checking to see if yal was alright cuz uh Billy Bob and err uhh Jeb here, theyz purty good mechanics. Well good night boss, yal be careful now.' And I said, 'Right. Good night, Bubba.'

Another time we were traveling out west and we stopped in a diner. Then some of those cowboy types with the shotguns in the back window of their pick-up trucks came up on us. There was just two of us in the restaurant dining, so they decided they were going to gang up on us. One of them went over to the bus and the dogs tried to jump through the window on them, growling and shit. Then they saw more of us in the bus; they burnt serious rubber getting the hell away from us. The bus was called the UJIBKUM CHARIOT, painted black and silver with gold highlights, and an Egyptian pyramid painted on the rear panel. Otherwise there were no names, slogans, symbols, or signs, because we wanted to be as low-key as possible. The bus was named after Lester's dog, Kummi and Roscoe's dog, Jibberimba.

Chicago: How do you feel with your life, your chosen path?
Moye: God bless the child that got his own. That's all I can say.

Chicago: For you, what is the meaning of Great Black Music—Ancient to the Future?
Moye: Total independence in a cooperative spirit of professionalism, research and artistic integrity to achieve ALL GOALS-RIGHTEOUSLY
—by any means necessary.

Chicago: Thank you
Moye: You're welcome.

VENTING FOR DON, LUBA, ARI AND KEN
Remembering Luba Raasheik and Ken Prince

Lincoln T. Beauchamp, Jr.
'Chicago Beau'

The art/life of Black people requires that it be curated by those who are of the Black Continuum and those who create out of kinship with the ancient forces. Here in **Jam For Your Life**, *African backbeat reaches forward and backward in an omnipresent collage of Black Diasporan musical spirituality.*

The drummers of the Simburu,
the great chanters of the Touareg,
the cries from the Middle Passage,
fertile Mississippi Delta yielding Black
blood enriched crops to a hungry greedy
white world, harmonicas made from
tobacco cans, hollow logs for playing
and sleeping, broomstick wire guitars
jammed on upside walls of share cropper
shacks, Macandal insighting insurrection
in Port-au-Prince, Harriet Tubman's
mighty underground railroad night
lighted by the brilliance of Ife,
lush life/night life ain't no good life/but/
it's my life/going down slow life/straight ahead life,
the grief at Gorée, the outlawed drum
which beats ever louder and
deeper in the souls of Black folk.

A billion sets of Black bones
rising out of the seas and soil
speaking through the music of
those of flesh and memory:

Jam For Your Life!

May 9, 1991

Written for the liner notes of Famoudou Don Moye's CD,
Jam For Your Life.

BLUES FOR ZAZEN
Joseph Jarman

Did you ever sit down
on a pillow that's round
and discover that you belong there.
That your heart and your soul
yes they are truly bold
you can live your life straight as an arrow.

You are right to the mark of the target
All the love in your heat it is pure
You are free in yourself as the air is!

Then you discover Blues for Zazen

You go on your way
living day after day
knowing all you need do is sit down
Everything that you feel
is a block in your path
and your reason for loving is sorrow.

And tho' no one speaks
as you go there
to the quiet place that's inside
you are all at One with the Heavens.

Even the Hell Gods let you pass by.

If you never sat down
on a pillow that's round
you may just be missing
a great pleasure.
Tho' it's hard when you start
to just simply sit down
you'll discover a joy
in your being.

Let the demons come
you'll destroy them.
Let the the terror grip
on your soul
Let the joy of life
enfold you!

Then you discover Blues for Zazen
Then you discover Blues for Zazen
Then you discover Blues for Zazen

JOSEPH JARMAN INTERVIEW

Lincoln T. Beauchamp, Jr.
'Chicago Beau'

25 April 1997
Brooklyn, New York

Chicago Beau: Where were you born, and when?
Joseph Jarman: September 13, 1937, Pine Bluff, Arkansas, the United States.

Chicago: From those humble beginnings in the South, how did you move into the world of music?
Joseph: Well, I was born in '37, and in '38 the family moved North to Chicago.

Chicago: How many in the family?
Joseph: Just my mom and me, and her baby sister, my auntie. Chicago promised work. They were coming out of The Depression, and building stuff for the War. So, we moved to Chicago. In Chicago, according to my best memory, my introduction to music came right after World War II when my uncles came home from the Service. I was seven or eight years old like that. They came home, and with them came Zoot Suits and Jazz music: Lester Young, Charlie Parker, Billie Holiday, they brought the culture into the family.

Chicago: Were you playing an instrument at that time?
Joseph: No.

Chicago: When did you get your first instrument?
Joseph: I didn't get my first instrument really until I got in High School. I was at DuSable High School in Chicago under the incredible guidance of Captain Walter Dyett who was the teacher of many famous musicians. In fact the thing I remember most in the music room is that Nat King Cole had carved his name into one of the desks. I started studying drums with Captain Dyett. I wanted to play saxophone, but the family couldn't afford to get me a saxophone, or wouldn't get me a saxophone. But originally I wanted a trumpet, and none of these things were possible. It was only in 1956 that I got my hands on a saxophone; it was a plastic saxophone. In 1956 I was in Germany in the Army. I was 18 years old. I had many friends there. On the weekends we would go into town to the Jazz clubs and the musicians from the various Army bands in the area would be in there playing. I met a lot of them, and actually started playing in those sessions with them, though not very good. At least I had the audacity and nerve to get up there. And I was also taking lessons with a German teacher. I practiced and studied with him for a year, and he taught me some good stuff. A little later on, in '57, I got transferred to the 11th Airborne Division Band, and I couldn't hardly play a lick. I got transferred through the system because

some friends of mine worked in the area where they made files, so they just made me a file and transferred me out.

When I got transferred into the band, the band director gave me sixty days to be able to play the basic marches. So the musicians in there, all of these men, from seven in the morning until midnight, would be on my case, and that was the greatest time, because I didn't have but sixty days to get my stuff together. The band director knew I couldn't play when I got there, so I had to learn. Otherwise, he was going to throw me out. So, I made it. At the end of the sixty days I was able to read the music and play the marches and stuff. I continued to play in the Jam Sessions and stuff. Then I got a temporary duty assignment with a trio to go around to Non-commissioned Officers Clubs and occasionally, Commissioned Officers Clubs in Frankfurt. I went to hear the 7th Army Jazz Band, Eddie Harris was in that band. And there was a very famous trumpet player in that band, the guy who wrote the music for 'The French Connection,' and there was bunches of guys in that band that are now connected with Hollywood, I see their names around every now and then.

Chicago: What year did you leave the Army?
Joseph: 1959.

Chicago: Did you go back to Chicago?
Joseph: Yeah, I went back. Because of various emotional problems, psychological problems, I didn't stay in Chicago. I drifted around the United States. I remember one night I was walking down a street in El Paso, Texas which was segregated back then, in fact it's still segregated. Anyway, I heard this saxophone coming from in this bar, so I went in there, and this saxophone player, an alto player, just blew me away. I'm trying to remember his name. It wasn't Cleanhead Vinson, but he was that style: really powerful, heavy alto, Texas Blues. And that sort of 'BOOM,' opened me up. It was a signal that this was the thing for me to do. So after that I went to Milwaukee, and after Milwaukee I went to Chicago and enrolled in Wilson Junior College. That's where I met Roscoe Mitchell, Jack deJohnette, Malachi Favors, Henry Threadgill, a bunch of cats. What is really important is that Malachi was a great musician to me. And Muhal Richard Abrams and Steve McCall . . . these were legends. These were the hard core guys. Yeah, and Anthony Braxton was there.

One day Roscoe invited to go to the Abraham Lincoln Center at Oakwood Blvd. and Langley Ave. They had an experimental band there that Muhal was running. First I was kind of tentative. I didn't really want to do it, I was afraid. But they accepted me quite well, and Muhal said something that lasted until this day with me, because I was withdrawn and afraid to contribute. The idea of that band was that everybody had an opportunity to write music and the band would play it. It wasn't for anything else. It didn't have an emotional, or material purpose. It was purely for the music, that's the only reason it existed. During that time I had said something to him about the music and he said to me: 'Write it, and one day it will be played.'

Even more importantly, Muhal invited me to his house. And Raphael Donald Garrett would be there. They would be playing. He invited me over there to play with them. I was scared to death. Raphael would ad-lib the saxophone part or the horn part as he played. I would be hearing him and Muhal, then I would be playing parallel to them. The proof of the benefit is that every Sunday we would go to this place called Flip Jacks and play. If you was good the people would give you a 'thumbs-up yay-yeah,' if you was bad, 'boo, boo' and you'd have to leave the stage. Von Freeman is the only person that carries that same tradition as far as I know in Chicago today. Fred Anderson carries that tradition, but because his orientation is different, he is like the evolution. I'm talking about the social setting for sessions. I always had a problem because I was moving always away from the norm, I did not want to play the changes. That's one of the things about the Art Ensemble, Lester used to insist on playing you know: 'You ain't playin the changes.' Sometimes I would get mad and play the changes real strict and get compliments from Malachi, 'That was real good,' he'd whisper to me. But I was never really interested in that particular approach. I was more psychologically oriented toward the concepts of later Coltrane, Dolphy, and Coleman as a philosophical/psychological approach to what music is about.

Chicago: And the Roscoe Mitchell Art Ensemble?
Joseph: I never knew it was called the Roscoe Mitchell Art Ensemble. That's always been controversial to me ever since the beginning. One thing prior to that that's real important is that Roscoe, Henry Threadgill, a piano player, bass player, drummer, and I, every Saturday would go to Roscoe's house and play. We were wanna-be clones of Art Blakey's Jazz Messengers. We actually had a gig at the school playing that material. And that was the greatest thing because we really weren't professionals at that time. I guess some of us were, but 98 percent of us were not.

Chicago: When was this?
Joseph: This was early 60s.

Chicago: So this is pre AACM?
Joseph: What happened is that there was an invitation to Phil Koran's house who was an organizer and activist, for a meeting. Because during that time there was tremendous upheaval, and tremendous Black consciousness. They had the idea to form an organization because the music we were playing, you couldn't go into a regular bar and play. And this organization was formed, The Association for the Advancement of Creative Musicians. Its purpose was to give each other respect and support, and to give us the opportunity to play our music on a public forum without the constraints of the general business community. We could develop our own audiences. We could play as long as we liked, whatever we wanted. Nobody would be drunk or demanding that you play this or that. So the concert format began to develop. It was very positive and very exciting for everyone. We would rotate the groups so that everybody had an opportunity to perform. I was fortunate. I was selected along with Fred Anderson's group, and Phil Koran's group to play the first concert at our new place, a rented hall on South Chicago Avenue.

Chicago: You guys were all heroes to us. We'd go and hear ya'l around University of Chicago, Ida Noyes Hall and places. Plus you guys had chicks, and you all were like a few years older, and playing some hip music, so we were real impressed.

Joseph: That was all right, all the same story sometimes. We had guys we were in awe of too.

Chicago: When did the Art Ensemble idea come into being?

Joseph: Groups had been formed. Roscoe was playing with Philip Wilson and Lester Bowie. That was the Roscoe Mitchell Ensemble. I was playing with Christopher Gaddie, Charles Clark, Thur Barker, Steve McCall, and Fred Anderson, sometimes. Then Delmark made the first AACM recordings. Muhal, Braxton, Mitchell, Jarman. After that, Christopher passed away from having his liver and kidneys all messed up in the army. Eight to fourteen months later, Charles Clark passed away from a brain hemorrhage. I was devastated. This absolutely crushed me. I mean we did our thing everyday. We would play for several hours everyday.

About six months after Charles passed away, Roscoe and Lester called me. Lester had one of those Delmark sessions. I believe to this day they called me to help me, because they sure didn't need me. I mean they were SMOKING. Lester invited me to play on his *Numbers 1 & 2*. We had a good time doing that, then they invited me to play a concert with them. And then very rapidly, if I did a concert I would ask them to play. If Lester did a concert, he would ask me to play. The same with Roscoe, if he did a concert, he'd ask us to play. There was no specific name. One day Lester, who had been interim AACM president at that time, pulled out a bunch of 100 dollar bills and said, 'You wanna go to Europe with us?' Lester is a funny guy, so he had to make it dramatic. I was alone. I didn't have anything to lose. I was struggling to survive. The next day I said yes. And we had a great time preparing to leave. I believe I have 8mm film footage of us preparing to leave. Then we went to New York and got on the USS United States liner and went across to France. We stayed several weeks in Place St. Michel in a little hotel that's not there anymore. It was all extremely exciting. As soon as we got there this French guy, Claude Delcoo, had arranged for a few simple gigs, nothing big. And because of the concentration, effort, and conviction the AACM had given us, the positive energy, we just did our thing; and fortunately it was well received. France itself was going through political and social changes. The old-line was getting old, and the new-line was coming in. The line of Americans that were coming in had all been conditioned by the changes on the American scene. So they were game to go all the way out. There were Blues guys there, Jazz guys there, painters, writers, poets. Everybody welcomed us. And Memphis Slim with his Rolls Royce. He was a regular guy. He would come up to me: 'Hello Joe,' very dignified, but warm like a brother. He was such a royal guy. You just dug the recognition from him, a master like that. In America, the famous never spoke to us. They would put us down as a matter of fact: 'You guys ain't playing shit.' There, in Paris, Memphis Slim came to several Art Ensemble concerts, and he would say: 'Um hum, yes!' He would never say thumbs down. And for him to give us his OK, we felt like, wow! We are doing something!

Chicago: Tell me about the mental institution yal stayed at.
Joseph: As I recall, a person at one of the concerts was a doctor, and he said they had space at this insane asylum. It was probably illegal but we didn't care. I remember Alan Silva had stayed there. Becky Friend had stayed there. I recall we were out of funds, and staying there gave us an opportunity to gather some bucks. We stayed there and they would have lunch everyday; and that's where my alcoholism began to manifest itself. At lunch time we would drink wine and cognac. And all the doctors would drink wine and cognac. We would have lunch and dinner with them. We could go in and out of that hospital, and you'd see the patients wandering around. We were like patients too—it was weird. There were some restrictions there, but we were able to handle it. I remember this one woman used to walk past our room and glare in. Bizarre. It was kind of interesting because we saw how the French were treating their mentally ill people. And they were treating them OK. Better than the Americans were treating theirs. Then we moved from there back to another hotel. I remember when we moved to St. Leu La Forêt, we had been living in St. Germain des Prés somewhere. Steve McCall was going to guide us out there, we had a Volkswagen van, and he didn't know where he was going. We went in a circle. He was talking about he was speaking French. All he could say was bonjour, and stuff like that. That was humorous. When we got out there we had a meeting, and it was at that time that the decision was made to refer to the group as the Art Ensemble of Chicago; because we were from Chicago, and we were an Art Ensemble. I don't know if Roscoe Mitchell had an Art Ensemble before that. I'd like to do paper work on that, because individuals' memories always expand what they want to expand, and that always alters the truth of history. It would be better to find out exactly when that name was used. We were having this meeting, and I believe it was Lester who said, 'Chicago.' It was just like in the movies. We were sitting around having a discussion, and we agreed. Everybody raised up their glasses of wine and saluted: ART ENSEMBLE OF CHICAGO FOREVER! That was kind of camaraderie and commitment. The decision was made there, I do know that. Immediately after that, it was in all the papers, along with all the controversy, ART ENSEMBLE OF CHICAGO IN EUROPE.

Chicago: Has the public sometimes misconstrued the meaning of your presentations, I mean political and not musical?
Joseph: That always came up because of the political environment of the times. But the Art Ensemble's motive actually, and this has been documented, wasn't that. We incorporated theatrical elements. We gave a definition of the costumes, based upon the personalities of what each individual wore. But if you look at the spectrum, we were representing history, from the 'Ancient to the Future.' And that slogan came from that realization. Malachi always represents the oldest entity because he would always wear these long full flowing robes. And he would look like an African/Egyptian Shaman. His persona would emulate that, and his music

and his style. He is very ancient. Then Moye was really in the midst of the African tradition. His drumming, his style, his approach, his feeling and his interests, were not a single African tradition, but a total African tradition. And still he had the entity of the African musical healer, a Shaman. I always perceived Don as 'Shamanistic.' My position was more moving toward the contemporary. I was Eastern oriented. These three were the pantheistic element of Africa and Asia. Roscoe represented the main-stream sort of Shaman, the Urban Delivery Man, delivering healing qualities. I love that photograph of him with the knife and the dice. The knife and the dice image looks like the gambler, or the trickster, or the prankster; but actually it's giving the chance to gamble for a living. And the fact that he's dressed up in such a nice suit means that it's possible to succeed with the threat and the gamble of living. Lester was always the investigator, wearing cook clothes, which is healing, creating energy and food. Then he advanced his awareness and went to the doctor's experimental laboratory. All of this Black imagery going from the 'Ancient to the Future' is represented in this stage attire. This is the way I perceived it, and all of our work had positive Kototama, which is a Japanese word that means magical sound, working toward communication. All of these people at some time or another had become aware of some kind of mystical communication between earth, energy, and music. Even though it was perceived because of the theatrics and the actual sound of the music itself, who would consider these (Jarman demonstrates tings, bells etc.) as viable musical instruments, given the restrictions of traditionalism. And one of the things, one of the elements that made the Art Ensemble search so diligently, was for the manifestation of the true sound. So that's why we had so many instruments. They were looking for specific sounds to express the music that was flowing through their consciousness. And that sound could be a bowl, a table, a piece of wood; whatever it took. Also there was another challenge with form, because the responsibility of form required the group to investigate an infinite number of forms. We were not masters of every form, but we certainly had to be aware of every form. For example, African forms of music. Moye would teach us African rhythms with specific forms. And get very annoyed, not that we didn't do it, but we didn't practice it the way he showed us, because of specific tradition. And he could do it. When we worked on it and did it right, you could feel the spirit click in, you could feel the spiritual uplift of the universality of the music. Even if it was a South East Asian form, when we got to the right level of that, you could feel the spirit click in.

Chicago: If you multiplied what you just said by some infinite number, you would approach an infinite variety in Art Ensemble concerts, and all of the collaborations with orchestras, dancers, the Zulu Chorus, etc.

Joseph: Exactly. One of the more interesting collaborations happened when we were back in Paris, and we were asked to do a soundtrack for a movie, *Crescendo*. Well, we did one movie soundtrack, *Les Stances à Sophie*, and that went really well. That was with Bridgitte Fontaine and Areski. But for this other film, Roscoe had written a piece for orchestra for that film. So they hired one of the Paris well known classical orchestras to play the score. They refused. They started to play it, but some of the orchestra members were too haughty, too stuck-up to play it. Ornette Coleman had that same experience in the past. But, in our case, beautiful, student musicians, graduate students, from one of the music schools in Paris, came in and SMOKED! So actually it was a great fortune for us that those old snobs didn't want to do it, cause the young people came in and did a beautiful job. That was the first collaboration that I recall. That was in 1970 I believe. There have many since then.

Chicago: You were with the group for how many years?
Joseph: From the beginning until 1993.

Chicago: The Art Ensemble was a big part of your life. For the most part, does the experience give you a good feeling?
Joseph: Not for the most part, for the total part. If you want to talk about music, I mean, THAT'S IT. Even the worst music performance of the Art Ensemble was a great musical performance to me. By worst musical performance, I mean the energy was not syncing, we were not in agreement with the form of what was going on, and the music would not work for us. But the audience, even if they did not become overwhelmed, they would enjoy, because there was at least that level of professionalism. The only time that I had a bad time with the Art Ensemble music was when I got drunk once in Belgium, and got fined fifty dollars for playing drunk on the stage. So that's the only annoying time I ever had. And they did it good to me. They said they didn't care if I got drunk, just don't get drunk on the stage and mess up the music. Of course the fifty dollar fine registered as a kind of humiliation, and it also registered sublimely that, I don't want to get drunk any more, because I don't want to pay fifty dollars. I might have gotten a little drunk after that but not enough to pay fifty dollars. So, I never had a negative experience. My decision not to perform with the Art Ensemble had nothing to do with the actuality of the music itself. Well, it may be about music, but it wasn't about the actuality of the music itself. It wasn't about actual playing.

Chicago: Your separation from the Art Ensemble was really a personal issue?
Joseph: Yeah, it's a personal issue. Plus it's a vibration that I don't want to put into the universe. It has been put there enough already. Whether it's true or false from my perspective, the energy goes into the blended energy of every living thing, and it will have some kind of effect. So rather than create effect based upon that information, I would prefer to create effect based on all of the wonderful, beautiful, positive experiences that happened. Any non-positive experience that happened will filter down, if necessary, to be reported upon. And you will come to your conclusion, you will realize something—this and that. I don't think any non-positive element can come in an objectively researched situation.

Chicago: It will have to be reversed anyway.
Jarman: Yes.

LARRY STEVENSON INTERVIEW

Lincoln T. Beauchamp, Jr.
'Chicago Beau'

Larry Stevenson, the son of Fontella Bass and Lester Bowie, has been a part of the Art Ensemble picture since he was nine years old. He has been a technician with the Art Ensemble and other AEC splinter groups for twenty years. What follows are some of Larry's thoughts on those who have so greatly influenced his life.

Chicago Beau: Larry, your thoughts and comments on your childhood in Paris, and experiences with the Art Ensemble cats.
Larry Stevenson: Growing up with these cats was an experience in itself. And with me being so young to start that experience, I was prime for learning.

Chicago: How old were you in the early days?
Larry: We went over there when I was nine years old and came back when I was eleven, almost twelve. It was heavy culture shock for me because by me going to American schools, and then all of a sudden one day you look up and you're moving to France and going to French schools; and not really realizing that you are moving to a different country. Because when you're so young you don't think about it like that. I'm moving to France! You don't even know where the hell that is. So when I got over there it was like, wow, this shit is different. And then all of a sudden the next thing I know I was in school and not speaking the language, but I adapted pretty well.

Chicago: You did learn how to speak French eventually?
Larry: Exactly. Just by being around the cats and being in school I was able to pick up the language pretty quick. Within six months I had picked up the language.

Chicago: Kids can be pretty tough anyway. If you don't speak the language and you're a blood, you were probably in for some challenges.
Larry: Right, that's what happened. I had to defend myself quite a few times. There were only two other Blacks living in this small town; and they had been adopted or something like that because they were with French families. They were two girls. There were no Black boys. Only three Blacks in total, but the strange thing is I went back last year and it's like Chinese, Blacks, all type of people in this town now.

Chicago: That's Sainte Leu la Forêt?
Larry: Yeah, it's looking like Paris.

Chicago: How do you feel about just growing up in a music family, and extended family.
Larry: It was a blessing really to grow up and live that. I don't think nobody's ever grown up like this. I mean, because everybody has been in musical families and stuff and had their different thing happening. But

being around so many different people and so many different characters—that was the incredible thing. And you got your mamma singing, you got your grandmamma singing, and then you got like a whole family, like a commune almost. In Europe sometimes we was living in tents, we were traveling around. They were trying to put out the message of the music and everything and we was living in tents for three months. Yeah, ma would be out there cooking, you know. Mom, I have to say, she was awfully brave.

Chicago: She was down with it?
Larry: Yeah, she was down with it. There's not too many women that would even do that.

Chicago: Hanging with her man, her peoples.
Larry: Yeah, right. That's what it was about, the family. And then it extended to the bigger family, which was the Art Ensemble. And, you know, it was all love in the house. And I really enjoyed seeing and feeling that. That's why I'm living over here in Europe now. I mean, that's part of the reason, because I really got to see what was happening in the world.

Chicago: A different vibe?
Larry: Ready for a different vibe, you know. I mean, by that I mean, these cats really exposed me to a lot of things in life that I can really see now. And I really thank them cats for that. I always tell them that, you know—because it's priceless.

Chicago: Absolutely priceless, man. Instead of living in your villa in Sardegna, you could have been warming yourself over an oil drum in a vacant lot in the Bronx. That could have been your world.
Larry: That's right. I feel really fortunate. My world, you know, is the whole world. By me being exposed to different cultures and stuff I feel like the whole world is my world; and if I want to go somewhere, I can just go. At the same time I don't forget my deep roots.

Chicago: We can't forget our original homes. No. We carry our roots with us.
Larry: You know. It's like I feel like the world is a part of us too; and wherever you go, you know, if you have it in you, you can go and do whatever it is. I'm telling you. But my thoughts from the Art Ensemble is that it's beautiful. They're, like I said, they brought me up the right way, really, by me living with these cats and enjoying the music. Like I can remember when Roscoe used to play for me on Christmas Eve. Cat used to play his bellaphone. Yeah. He still has it matter of fact. I think it's in the archives now.

Chicago: Well the cats weren't no babies when they went to Europe, so they had had many experiences before that.
Larry: Oh yeah. Some of the cats were military veterans, and had families and stuff. When I was eight them cats was like thirty-five and shit.

Chicago: They were already famous in Chicago; and Malachi was already a legend.
Larry: Yeah, and he's still hanging tough, boy. He's a good cat and a strong cat. He's the oldest cat, the elder.

Chicago: It's difficult for me to imagine a more ideal and balanced set of influences to be around as a child.
Larry: Like I said, I know I'm fortunate. And I'm happy in my life because I learned certain things from them at an early age. I really have them to thank.

Chicago: Thanks a lot, Larry.
Larry: You got it.

Larry Stevenson

REFLECTIONS ON PARIS:
Early Days of the Art Ensemble

Lincoln T. Beauchamp, Jr.
'Chicago Beau'

Africa is the home of the artist;
the only continent on this planet which is soul-possessed.
                                        Henry Miller

I arrived in Paris from Amsterdam in late August 1969. The scene was fertile with painters, writers, poets, dancers, and musicians. Everywhere change was in the air: change in attitudes, change in music, change in social mores. Nearly every creative act contained an element of revolution, protest, discontent, or an appeal for peace. The war in Viet Nam raged on. The populace in the United States were reeling from assassinations, civil protests, official-unofficial martial law, and the ever lengthening list of war dead. For many artists, the time had come for a respite from the day-to-day soul shattering existence in the United States.

Paris of the late Sixties and early Seventies served as a nurturing cauldron for artistic expression and ideas; and she was still a Euro-urban, cosmopolitan haven for senior creators like Beauford Delaney, Josephine Baker, Jean Paul Sartre, Aejo Carpentier, Leopold Senghor and others who brilliantly lit the scene with memory and presence.

On almost any evening one could find hanging out at the American Center, or the *Chat que Peche* and Storyville night clubs such notables as Mickey Baker, Hank Moble, Reverend Frank Wright, Earl Freeman, Sonny Sharock, Big Marva Broome, Sunny Maurry, Hart LeRoi Bibbs, Shirley Scott, Archie Shepp, Dexter Gordon, Anthony Braxton, Clifford Jordon, Memphis Slim, Johnny Griffin, Pablo Savage, Willie Mabon and members of the Art Ensemble of Chicago: Joseph Jarman, Malachi Favors, Lester Bowie, Famoudou Don Moye, and Roscoe Mitchell.

I heard the Art Ensemble play the first time before percussionist and drummer Famoudou Don Moye joined the group. I was part of the show. They invited me to play harmonica with them at a music Festival in Amougies, Belgium, in September 1969. I played one tune along with another guest harpist, Julio Finn, then I joined the audience to watch the remainder of the show that climaxed with Joseph Jarman removing a specially made red suit piece-by-piece and throwing it into the audience until he was completely naked. This occasion marked the beginning of what was to become a long and enduring relationship extending beyond music. The following year Famoudou Don Moye joined the group, and the five began their joyous, but not always easy task of being caretakers in the Black Continuum.

For two years the Art Ensemble lived in France, and performed throughout Europe. They were a major force in the vibrancy of Paris of that period, contributing enormously to that city's reputation as a cultural Mecca with their presence, numerous concerts, and recordings on French record labels.

They planted seeds that are still yielding a fruitful harvest; not only for themselves, but for so many who have come after them—and even for some that came before them.

For three decades the epigram of the Art Ensemble, 'Great Black Music! Ancient to the Future,' has been strictly adhered to. They are constantly and consistently contributing to the fabric of Black music, presenting the gamut of its history through their special projects such as: Art Ensemble of Chicago with the Dianne MacIntyre Dancers 1987; Art Ensemble of Chicago and the Woman of the Calabash 1991; Art Ensemble of Chicago/Soweto with the Amabutho Male Chorus 1992; Art Ensemble of Chicago with special guest, Don Pullen; Frankfort Jazz Festival 1992; Art Ensemble of Chicago and the Blues Tradition 1993; Art Ensemble of Chicago and Deutsche Kammerphilharmonie 1993.

The stage presentation of the Art Ensemble is a stunning resplendence of cymbals, chimes, percussions, saxophones, horns, drums, gongs, whistles, fabrics, feathers, and hand-fashioned instruments. They wear a variety of costumes and face paint.

Ancestor and Spirit possession, spontaneous preaching, teaching, dancing, poetry reading, chanting, moaning, praying, singing, screaming, humoring, and audience interactions have kept the Art Ensemble at the vanguard of music presentations.

Lester Bowie and Famoudou Don Moye receiving the 'Honorary Citizens Award,' from the Mayor of Caprarola, Italy, 1994

ART ENSEMBLE OF CHICAGO
THE BAND WHICH HAS GIVEN A NEW AND TOTALLY MUSICAL SIGNIFICANCE TO THE TERM, BLACK POWER

Mike Hennessey

In August 1966, the 26-year-old Chicago multi-instrumentalist, Roscoe Mitchell, recorded the album *Sound* for the Delmark label. In his sextet at the time were trumpeter Lester Bowie, also 26, from Frederick, Maryland, and 39-year-old Chicago bassist, Malachi Favors.

Nobody—not even the musicians themselves—had any intimation of it at the time, but that album planted a musical seed that was to flourish and flower into one of the most uniquely enterprising, adventurous, exploratory and creative groups in the history of Black Music: the Art Ensemble of Chicago.

Recalling the album, which appeared at a time when the Jazz movement was in something of an *avant garde* turmoil as jazz musicians energetically, stridently and anarchistically looked for new directions in which to take the music, British writer Graham Lock observed:

'Just when one wondered how jazz could go any further without smashing itself to pieces on walls of febrile noise, Roscoe Mitchell—practically unknown outside his native Chicago—reasserted the elementary values of space and silence. His *Sounds* and *Congliptious* LPs (the latter recorded for Nessa Records in March 1968, with Bowie, Favors, and drummer, Robert Crowder) signaled a new attitude in the music; it stopped screaming and began to breathe. *Sound* floated in and out of silence; cries and whispers would swell and fade in a complex ensemble dynamic.'

In between those two pacesetting albums, Bowie, Favors, and Mitchell joined the forces in the Lester Bowie Quartet for another Nessa date in August 1967, producing *Number 1/Number 2*. Completing the quartet on that occasion was 29-year-old multi-instrumentalist, Joseph Jarman, from Pine Bluff, Arkansas. These four men were the founding fathers of the Art Ensemble of Chicago—a group title foreshadowed by the name of the unit: The Roscoe Mitchell Art Ensemble.

Since those pioneering days, the Art Ensemble of Chicago has become a major force on the Jazz scene, expanding from a quartet to a quintet when drummer and percussionist Don Moye joined the group in Paris in 1969. Not the least impressive aspect of the remarkable AEC story is that it has survived and prospered with the same personnel for three decades—an astonishing and unprecedented achievement for a co-operative group which speaks volumes for the musical, mental, and moral compatibility of its members.

As British writer and musician Ian Carr has noted: 'The Art

Ensemble showed a way out of the cul-de-sac of abstraction and became one of the key groups of the 1970s and 1980s. Its inclusive, pluralistic music fused elements from free jazz and the whole jazz tradition, going back to New Orleans, and there were also strong ethnic—particularly African—ingredients. Their performances also presented the music with brilliant theatrica.'

Lester Bowie says: 'All the members of the Art Ensemble have special areas of expertise—so between us we can operate over a wide range of music. We have five different people with five different lives and sets of experiences which are brought in to make up the music. This isn't a band where a leader dictates the way everything should be done.'

In the course of its three decades of existence, the AEC has produced a richly varied pantheon of recorded music—more than forty albums, not counting a growing catalogue of bootlegs. The legitimate repertoire includes two seminal albums for ECM, *Nice Guys* and *Full Force*, and other landmark sessions for Delmark, Atlantic, Freedom, and, more recently, the Japanese DIW abel.

But the full impact of the Art Ensemble can only be experienced in live performances, with their colorful costumes, their tribal 'warpaint' and their immense panoply of percussion instruments.

The AEC has always proclaimed its repertoire as being 'Great Black Music: Ancient To The Future.' The fact that the Ensemble came into being in the mid-60s, at a time when the United States was in the throes of a civil rights upheaval, when Malcolm X's Black Nationalist movement was mounting a militant challenge to institutionalized racial discrimination, meant that the band was frequently identified with the Black Panthers and its members portrayed as angry, white-hating, politically-motivated renegades.

But, as Don Moye has observed: 'All the political agitation of the 60s is contained in part of who we are. They tried to involve us politically with slogans and rhetoric, but none of us had any background in the bullshit of politics. Our training was as musicians—we wanted to make strong musical statements about our identity and heritage. We wanted to make a strong declaration of who we were, regardless of the social climate—but we never got involved in the politics.'

British writer Valerie Wilmer succinctly identified the AEC's position in the hierarchy of Black American music when she wrote:

'The Art Ensemble are a long way from being revolutionaries in any political sense, and yet their music represents another interpretation of Black Power. Although the dedicated bunch of Chicagoans are artists first and foremost, they come closer to realizing that slogan than some of their brothers do, simply through playing the people's music.'

CELEBRATING THE ART ENSEMBLE OF CHICAGO

Isio Saba

March 1974, Bergamo Jazz Festival, the first I cover as journalist and photographer, my first meeting with the five 'magical' musicians of the ART ENSEMBLE of CHICAGO. I try to interview them, but I have to give up because Don Moye plays and jokes, remembering his past Roman holidays towards the end of the critical 60's: the places, the jazz people along the Tevere.

Anyway, that picture of mine of the AEC in Bergamo, which became the cover of Super Sound magazine, has become history for the Chicago musicians, and for me, as I was beginning a career as special reporter (not getting paid for it!) at a jazz festival.

Fascinated, surprised, involved by the music and by the theater of the Chicago band: I have no need to reread that which I wrote about them such a long time ago, exactly when critics were still unsure whether to label them clowns or musicians.

July '74, Pescara Jazz Festival: it's my second meeting with the AEC, which in this circumstance has as a special guest Muhal Richard Abrams, the pianist leader of AACM. Needless to say their style impresses me even in this circumstance. Same with the critics who, hearing them play 'standard' in a jam-session at a club, remain fascinated. Three years pass before I finally get to know them as friends.

It's the summer of '77, when Lester Bowie is passing through Rome on his way home from a trip to Africa where he had been guest of, and had played with, Fela Kuti. Lester is having financial problems, he's expecting money to come in from Chicago, but this money does not seem to be coming . . . so I invite him to stay at my place. I am still a journalist-photographer of no account, who loves music, but lives on another job.

Given the circumstances, Lester asks me to find some concerts, to introduce him to other musicians, to become his manager at least in Italy, and this is how the concerts of Agrigento, Modena, Livorno, Cagliari, Roma, came about. Bowie held these concerts together with young and promising Italian musicians of the most different musical backgrounds.

It's the beginning of a long story that sees Lester Bowie and the Chicagoans frequently meet musicians like Antonello Salis, Maurizio, Gianmarco, Massimo Urbani, Marcello Melis, and also Tullio de Piscopo, James Senese, Pino Daniele, Roberto Murolo, Beppe Barra, the best of Neapolitan music, the best of Sardinia's ethnic tradition, the Bitti Choir, and yet others of the most different musical orientations.

In '78-'79 I become the manager of Lester of the AEC. Sometimes the tours take us out of Italy too, with significant results concerning both the organizational level, and the image.

Important tours bring the Art Ensemble to sign a contract with ECM; and in '79 the album *Nice Guys* sees the light, and the cover picture is mine! The picture travels the world and becomes history; Roscoe Mitchell, Malachi Favors, Joseph Jarman, Don Moye, and Lester Bowie, sitting around a table at a bar of Piazza Pasquino; behind Vicolo dei Granari, where I've lived for years, near the splendid Piazza Navona: this is a mystic area at the centre of Rome, a reference point for the AEC in Italy, but maybe I shouldn't be the one to say this.

After the Parisian experience, which lasted to the end of the 60's, the AEC chooses Rome and Italy regularly as a European base of its past two decades.

I also want to recall Cagliari and a region ('Sardinia amore—full of lonely people') as one of the places that keeps on coming up in the recent history of the AEC; this island witnessed the meetings between the Chicago quintet and groups like, From the Roots to the Source, and Brass Fantasy, and then all of them together!

The AEC's history is also the history of all those groups that have rotated around, and still depend on, those five musicians that have chosen Chicago as an adoptive mother city, if not of birth.

Other pictures, thousands of pictures, black and white and color, all around Europe and the US: an unrepeatable history, made up of stage and backstage images, which tell the physical evolution and the changes in the look of these great musicians. These pictures can witness the musical evolution and a style, sometimes considered outdated and old, which is instead solid and effective today, as it has been for the past thirty years.

Avantgarde. Free. Tradition. The search for roots. Soul and rap. The AEC is this and much more. It isn't only Great Black Music, but also the meeting point between this and many other musical realities often unknown and to many, seemingly obscure.

Another photograph which made history sees the AEC with the South African group, Amabutho Male Chorus, during the Twenty-fifth Anniversary of the group 1990-1991. Another important encounter, documented by recordings and CDs that witness the vitality of the Chicago group and the opening towards their Soweto brothers.

These last years have witnessed maybe a slight change, a slowing down, in the activities of this group, due to choices made by the single players, choices which brought them to highlight their personal experiences (vital to the style of the AEC), so we have Brass Fantasy, New York Organ Ensemble, Leaders, From the Roots to the Source Sound Ensemble, Sun Percussion.

These experiences led us to think that the AEC was running out of reasons to remain a musical Ensemble with a something new to propose; instead, the concerts held towards the end of '94 and the beginning of '95 have scattered these ideas; the freshness, the modernity, the vitality, the inspiration of the group, all was fully recovered and shown.

Sometimes being emotionally close to a band makes one lose the real perspective on facts, both from the musical standpoint, and from the organizational level. With immense pleasure I could verify the real, concrete vitality of this group, which went beyond the rosiest expectations.

From New York to California; from Paris to Berlin; from Munich to Bologna; dozens of concerts in these last months, followed by an enthusiastic audience and critics; it seems like an old picture, seen again and again, slightly faded maybe; instead it's only the anticipation of the birthday party we'll have in a few months.

Today's AEC is missing Joseph Jarman, maybe only on a short leave, but the original value of the musical production hasn't changed. For them, the idea of getting together to celebrate their birthday, of commemorating with a revival a story which is over, is inconceivable.

The story is not over, and the picture of the Thirtieth Anniversary of the AEC will come in a few months, probably on a stage that will witness the triumph of instruments and percussions of different shapes and sizes, maybe there will be unexpected guests, anyhow, the true image will be that of an unrepeatable sound.

Seeing the technological advances, I wonder if in the future this image may be transmitted in its original color, music, shapes. I wonder if the magic of internet, of CD ROMs, of virtual reality, will be able to equal their imagination and creativity.

What will be the real image of the AEC after the year 2000? It's a good question, which stirs imagination; but I'd better return to the past!

A saying from my country says: 'There, where you hear music, stop: for music knows no enemies'. . . and the friends of AEC have often stopped in this, returning its hospitality with sounds and a brotherly touch.

Translated from the Italian by Paola Ciapanna

races places faces & asses

hartmut geerken

where the art ensemble of chicago begins most others have already ended the sound of the silent gongs to guide the people of the sun through grey haze fanfare for the warriors i met moye & bowie for the first time in athens (1982) & west africa then was a highlight (1985) with moye & tchicailolu & his whispering meditation ass who inspired famodou & me writing down all sort of shit on asses all around the world during breakfasts in sierra leone guinea & liberia here it is races places faces & asses the antidiluvial australian quasi pocket ass the amazing afrikan plateau ass &/or johannesburg table ass the all american full moon ass in black & white featuring the exclusively improving las vegas automatic plastic ass with holly-wood extensions the continuously spreading & overflowing bavarian malt ass called rotarsch the incredible mama roma hairy street pasta ass the so called british parliamentary commonwealth ordinary thatcher ass the aromatic & preferrably fried nice little french ass the general mongolian pardonable flat ass the subordinate japanese negative non ass the liberian undulating cassava green soft ass the gelatinous & transparent benelux pink ass the practical greek ten drachma acropolis anti turk ass the socialized bangourien robust guinean foo foo ass the squeaking sierra leonean rutile ass (for export only) the friendly neighborhood slamdunk double sleeper ass the incredible non resisting sweet & sour sometime casually disappearing scandinavian whispering ass (excepting finland) the commonmarket & nato so called disarmament european fat ass for an unhappy day i have jackson in my house actual two (1969) i listened to it for the first time in kabul afghanistan exactly three years after it was recorded in paris france dedicated to charles clark who passed away nine weeks before the album was done & he was twenty four years then ericka not to be mixed up with erika please child of our uncharted microtones thrown through the dawn the maze of longing as she matures in black america the panther paying homage to the people torn with the gun television hero gone to madness seeking the answer no description of the tones please roscoe malachi with the brain of a japanese kabuki musician close to satori & lester looks at you with dali eyes frontal as i mentioned a jackson in your house when june tyson & pat patrick were at my place in heliopolis egypt there was a big laughter & june said that's too baaaad for another unhappy day i have message to our folks actual twenty eight (1969) lesterroscoejosephmalachi with old time religion dexterity as good as bird joseph with the bible in his hand already on his way to the ny zen monastery fingers full of rings roscoe with a smart suit a flash tie ritzy shoes a knife in his right two loaded dice in his left hand lester wears tuxedo the safety catch of his gun released the horn in his left malachi this time a japanese rice field worker with his shovel our hope/love only yet-HE-the messenger homeless sage-seer in blood color these hollow cities of europe as well as actual twenty nine reese & the smooth ones (1969) recorded the same day after null sonne no point (1996) i was very astonished re-listening to mandel hall recorded on my twentythird birthday or kush after many years the pulse on sun ra's sun harp with the far eastern sticks & the pulses there on delmark & diw the always diligent moye between jetlag & overfatigue the long lasting sheets of sound of the 80s the repeatedly shouted structured signals of the 90s you would buy all their stuff without listening to in the next century gittin' to know y'all (1969) was one of the pieces played over & over again during years surrounded by desert sands on makattam egypt with open windows towards the pyramids & with closed eyes terribly loud phones on the ears the bumble bees for starting with bowie could be good (sometimes) being backed by europeans with one single note only (but not the one coming from whispering ass) the three drummers the one trumpet & the voice of the one trumpeter where are the rest of the voices WHERE ARE THEY let's hear the voices lester's conducting belly voice whipping european brain technicians lester's voice the red thread through gittin' to know y'all i don't know today what was yesterday it's nighttime & the dogs are praying you're sleeping under my weight you don't play the kongoma with your trumpetfingers i said to lester & he agreed immediately roscoe asked do you think it's alright like that & i answered yes it's cool lester's tp & cigar in his left hand the right busy with the valves his knuckles nudge in roscoe's nostrils but roscoe seems unimpressionable his legs working in schwaz long time alternatively standing on tiptoe or heels the right foot long time nestles behind the left one time he straddles the right leg for long time then he stands on it for long time in a balancing act all movements of his legs & arms suggest that he's rehearsing take off with subsequent soar for decades as soon as lester pointed his jet towards the audience a tremendous cloud of garlic came over the listeners the waitawhile produced garlic schnaps after the red & white balloon has disappeared between the stars joseph was still standing & looking he said although the balloon disappeared i can see it if i want to it depends on me & my concentration only during flatus de frappe famoudou & i were stating if there was material or not most of the time we articulated the word material simultaneously with big laughter what's that thing called certain blacks certain blacks twentyfour minutes they do what they wanna & on the flip side one for jarman & bye bye baby very strange indications on jacket & label mr lester bowie & mr edward mitchell jr but we know it better multiinstrumentalist chicago beau guides the boat as it lifts off from the realm of earthly beauties & nastiness into other dimensions & spaces where there is no difference anymore between life & evil all america jackets & labels are sloppy full of misprints the very first lp i got was nessa one followed by nessa two with robert crowder & others far out solos tutankhamen & congliptious/old recorded little more than a year after i arrived in egypt everybody should be able to carry the music alone to be continued with people in sorrow did you hear the silence lately you think your phonograph has gone but finally there are some bells the bass the chimes the little gongs the bell clusters metal only madly sunny sun rays reflect on raindrops somewhere sometimes very close to an afternoon of a georgian faun temple blocks only the definite bass introduces lester's sorrow a kissing trumpet a spitting trumpet a sucking trumpet did you eve kiss a trumpet mouthpiece the flute directs far east lester speaks more clear now he catfoots towards malachi muted horn clear tamourin penetrates everything fuck stockhausen & his retinue for those moments a police whistle pours oil on troubled water & it's like at the beginning the rising at the end & the flying & the landing.

REFLECTIONS OF JAMAICA

DonAlonzo Beauchamp

Jamaica. In one word was, is, and will always be TIAMO, the name of the AEC Jamaican compound. Realizing what it means to be asked to express the recollections of any of my experiences with the Art Ensemble might be as humbling as it is to realize what it means to have these experiences and share to life with this momentous occasion, GREAT BLACK MUSIC - ANCIENT TO THE FUTURE. I am DonAlonzo, and for me to reflect on Jamaica specifically, is difficult because it is impossible to capsulise one particular assignment and separate it from the role it plays in a long stream of overlapping events that define my life in the service of the AEC. However, the richness of the atmosphere created in Jamaica provided the perfect demonstration of many things that the AEC is really about. Jamaica was about family. Lester's wife, Deborah, came, as well as his daughters Zola and Sukari. His son, Bahnamous, was there working with me as the crew. Moye had his wife, Gloria, and son, Adama, there. Roscoe was accompanied by his woman, Wendy, and his daughter, Attala. It was interesting to see the group with their families.

For the first time, I had the chance to see the AEC operate the way it was intended to. I began to understand an important element in the root of what the AEC is creating. Cohabitation clearly put them in their natural state of mind and they worked together so comfortably that they were able to let the music make all the decisions. It was pure inspiration. Everybody knew their function instinctively and exercised it in the same manner. I was responsible for receiving the cargo, setting up the instruments, airport pick-ups and drop-offs, and driving locally for any number of various errands.

To receive the cargo was to be subjected to the backwards UK inspired bureaucracy of a third world country. I had no idea what I was in for. I was used to the backwards bureaucracy of America and its European counterparts, but this was a whole new game. It took several trips, hours of lines, every form thinkable of the run-around, a few payoffs, and a quick self education on how to command your turn amidst a ruthless mob of aggressive masters of this skill. I maneuvered through all of this with Bahnamous. Together, we were able to support each other through these ordeals with the overstanding that we would ultimately arrive at appreciation for them. We even got shook down by two soldiers from the Jamaican Army with M-16s. They were particularly hard on me. I tightened my stomach in anticipation of the gut shot that I knew was coming because his interrogation was right out of a movie where the next move was the butt of a rifle taking the wind out of me. It never happened, but we had good laughs about the incident later. Our commitment to each other and our cause resulted in the successful receipt of the cargo.

Once we got the instruments, it was time to set them up. This was not difficult, considering the fact that we were used to setting up the instruments every night. In fact, we were able to take our time and tend to some long awaited fine tuning of both the instruments and cases. It was interesting to see how much care they put into their equipment when the conditions allowed them to do so.

The airport runs were actually day long adventures where anything could happen.

First of all, the steering wheel was on the right side and people drove on the opposite side of the street than I was used to. It took me a little longer to get used to driving than it took Bahnamous, but eventually, we became pros at the two hour each way trip to the airport in Kingston. Passing through all the towns on the way, diggin those fine Jamaican sisters diggin us as we passed by, trying to avoid the hazards of the Jamaican roads, trying not to be a hazard to the people that aren't used to us moving through their life, lunch stops at Boston Beach or one of the towns, seeing the coastline from the top of the mountains, the waterfalls, the trees. All of these things made the airport runs adventurous, but for the most part, we just wanted to make it there and back! Then we could enjoy the adventure.

The local trips became more interesting the longer we stayed, because the longer we stayed the more people we knew. The more people we knew, the more we had to do. At first, most of the local trips were to the market for Rocky or Ivy. Rocky was the man in charge of the property, and Ivy was the cook. We would often bring them home in the evening, as well as any of the staff members. I really enjoyed the relationship with the staff. It was kind of awkward for them at first because they never had to work for Black people, but since we were there working too, they realized that their job was to work with us and be themselves. Aron was the youngest of the staff and he took us to the Roof, a dance hall club, on the first night. After that, trips to the Roof became a just as regular as the market. However, I had to leave the Roof alone for a while because I had a jealous Jamaican girl after me. She even threatened to kill this white girl from Toronto if she caught her touching me. I found the whole thing rather funny, but the girl from Toronto was terrified. We caused a whole scene, so I stayed away from the Roof for about a week.

As I mentioned, at first the local driving was basically the routine trips that it takes to keep everything running smooth, but it didn't take long for Moye to tap into the scene and have a million things to do. He vigorously went after everything that Jamaica had to offer him, and offered everything he had with the same intensity. He was on a mission to continue his search to expand his vocabulary with the drum. He submerged himself in Kumina culture and brought it back to all of us. I often had to make trips into Breastworks to pick the Kumina drummers up and bring them to play at Tiamo. They would always have some kind of unexpected stop to make or person to take somewhere, stop over here, pick this up, drop that off over there, etc. There was always much confusion, usually brought about by Prophet Salaam, probably the most spirited of the drummers, but I was able to prevent them from altering the plan too much because it was my duty to follow the instructions that Moye gave me. King Koot, or Whitebeard as some called him, was the man in charge and he respected my conviction to carry out orders, but insisted that I didn't have to worry so much about it.

After a few weeks, there was more than enough music for the ODWALLA project, and it was time to pack up the instruments and bring them to the studio, which was at Irie Beach, just outside of Ocho Rios, about two hours away. We left them at the studio and basically commuted for the first couple of sessions. For this, it was necessary that we have another vehicle, so we ended up hiring Courtney, who had a cab service, to work with us. We brought Courtney into our program, and he fit so perfectly, it was like having another crew member. He, like the staff at Tiamo and many people that work closely with the AEC, realized that the whole idea is to do your job and all the experiences are shared with you like everyone else.

In fact I consider it to be part of my responsibility to recognize that and enjoy it.

There was a lot of orientation with the studio. A whole new staff that quickly picked up on the fact that we expected them to work with us, more than for us. Of course everyone has to follow orders and do their job, but it's about sharing life. Mikey ran the studio, which was just a small part of the land he owned. There were waterfalls and an organic farm. One of the cats that worked there named Aron became known as the Ital Chef because he hooked up a delicious plate of boch choy and beans. He even made up a song about it while freestyling to the music of Big Red Peaches (one of the songs that was being recorded). He was very talented, and we agreed to look for the opportunity to work together in the future. The engineer was Paul and his assistant was Dwayne. Neither of them had ever dealt with anything like this, and it took a little time for them to adjust to a new set of rules, but once they got past the idea of that, they were able to apply their expertise with the proper direction, and before too long, we were in full swing.

At first we would go to the studio for a day, and then go back to Port Antonio, but we ended up staying close to the studio for a couple days at a time so that we could go straight to the studio without having to deal with the long drive. Towards the completion of the project, their families started leaving, and it was decided that we would stay close to the studio until the project was finished. Relocating to Ocho Rios exposed me to a whole new area of Jamaica, and being close to the studio everyday allowed us to get down and concentrate fully on the project. It was the first time I had been involved with the production of an Art Ensemble record and I enjoyed watching, learning, and participating in yet another facet of the music business using the AEC method.

With the music recorded, it was time to pack up the instruments, and once again deal with Jamaican customs to ship everything back. This time we shipped everything from Montego Bay. The airport there is a little more modern, and caters to the general tourist scene, so the run-around wasn't as long, but of course, we had to go through the same drawn out process to get the instruments out as well. The pressure to receive them was a lot less serious because they had served their purpose for this project, and anything that happened to them would not affect our direction at that time. However, my concern wasn't over until I picked them up in Chicago.

After a few days of mixing, the project was complete, and we went on to the next phase of activity. All in all, through all the complications and amidst all the craziness, looking back on the Jamaican project, it seems to have flowed so easily and naturally. I guess that is the result of hard work paying off, a big part of what makes working for the Art Ensemble so rewarding. It is the way that GREAT BLACK MUSIC - ANCIENT TO THE FUTURE works.

PRAISES FROM FRIENDS AND COLLEAGUES

'They [Art Ensemble of Chicago] are very creative. They are revolutionary. Their things are so different that they open up most musicians' ears as to the possibilities of what to do with the music. They have been together over thirty years, and that's as remarkable and right on as their music.'

Mal Waldron, musician

* * *

'The first time I heard them I knew they had something important to say, and say it for a long time.'

Maurice Culloz, Radio France

* * *

'The Art Ensemble is one of the most important groups of the last part of the Twentieth Century, one of the most important groups in modern music because of certain musical and artistic innovations. Their thing is a whole situation: from musical to spiritual, to life itself. I consider the Art Ensemble the primary group of the last part of this century. To give to people such a large, varied, and beautiful palette of creation; I can't think of anybody else that's done that.'

'The caliber of musicians in the Art Ensemble is outstanding. They are Motherfuckers! I have to use that word. They are Motherfuckers! They are playing their asses off; and what they are playing is so important. The visual aspect of their presentation is as incredible as hearing them. When you hear them—the phrasing, etc. All put together, they are Motherfuckers!'

Steve Potts, musician

* * *

'What stands out in my mind about the Art Ensemble besides the obvious innovations they made and continue to make, is the fact that they've stayed together. When you consider the odds, the obstacles and the forces leveled against an institution like that, just in terms of art itself, to say nothing about the social ramifications; that makes them a phenomenon on two levels: a musical, and a social level. The implication here is that there is an incredible high level of intelligence going on between these guys. To be able to see—to visualize the obstacles and persevere. These guys are a positive and inspiring institution.'

Billy Hart, musician

* * *

'All the musicians in the Art Ensemble, they're very serious about their music, they're constantly enlarging their whole musical experiences and outlook about things. I mean, these guys not only love jazz music, they study classical art forms from all over the planet. You know, it's something else. You have to love each other and really appreciate each other's individual talents to really stick together.'

'It's very hard to find people in any kind of business that want to really stick together and do something and have commitment towards a certain goal. Cause, I mean, most people are not that strong of character. These guys got such character, yeah.'

Ari Brown, musician, and AEC substitute

* * *

'I remember the first concert we did with the Art Ensemble was in Queen Elizabeth Hall. The thing that just grabbed me so much about the group was that they had such a sense of theater and drama. The way they attacked music and told a story through a concert. It's a very rare skill and talent. The Art Ensemble always struck me as more than just a group of musicians performing in a recognized format. They've got this tweak about their work which is a love of tradition going way back. They use tradition to inform the future. Their tag line, *Ancient to the Future,* is very cleverly thought through. It's always a pleasure working with them because you know that what you get is something no one else can do. I mean there is an extraordinary buzz on stage sometimes that nobody else can do. Moye and Malachi are exceptional. It's exceptional the way they each have their own persona on stage. . . it's very rare. And each time they play, one senses their commitment, just from their presence on stage, and from the very first note.'

John Cummings, promoter

* * *

'A rich and multi-faceted flame, at once impeccably classic and ultra-modern—such is the music of the Art Ensemble of Chicago. They fill space with their sumptuous tapestry; the rhythm is ever-present, even during the moments of 'silence'; uplifting and joyful. Playing at hide-and-seek, at piggy-back jumping, at swinging around the maypole, and at blindman's bluff, they are like a tranquil and sun-kissed lake, like a triumphant rainbow. They resemble nothing and no one else, but are uniquely themselves, united and yet different, everyone of them is full of striking colors. Sometimes almost tough, sometimes lyrical, they are at once as creative as children, and masters in complete control of their art.

To them respect and affection.'

Brigitte Fontaine

PS. Love and kisses to everybody,

Brigitte

Translated from the French by Julio Finn

ODWALLA

Joseph Jarman

ODWALLA came through the people of the Sun
into the grey haze of the ghost worlds
vanished legions, crowding breadlines - the people
of the Sun coated with green chalk
all kinds of warm light between them
destroyed for the silver queen of the ghost worlds
wild beast such as dogs gone mad and lechers-wanderers

ODWALLA came through the people of the Sun
to warn them of vanished legions
and to teach them how they may increase their bounty
through the practice of the drum and silent gong
(as taught by ODWALLA) was realized

on seeing one another they transformed themselves into
one the hand the other the left big toe of KAW ZU PAM
(the one who creates the door through the passage on the hill of
QUAN BU KA) their purpose
to guide the people of the Sun as they sought
knowledge of
the door through the grey haze

when SEKA saw the sound of the silent gong
SEKA sought to transform itself into the right hand
of ODWALLA where COO BE SU rested while
waiting

to move into the right toe of KAW ZU PAM
(the one who creates the door through the passage
on the hill of
QUAN BU KA) their purpose
to guide the people of the Sun as they
seek to leave, seek to leave, seek to leave, seek to leave
the grey haze

only RIMUMBA remained to find the place of the
drum and silent gong
such knowledge would enable it to enter into the inner
organs of
KAW ZU PAM
(the one who creates the door through the passage on the hill of
QUAN BU KA) their purpose
to guide the people of the Sun the grey haze

ODWALLA vibrated the movement of CAM BE GILL O POIU
causing the silent gong to sound silent
the body whole

the grey haze Sun people drum
Silent gong—here now
here now—between us
grey haze Sun
people

ART ENSEMBLE OF CHICAGO
Selected Discography

Sound
The Roscoe Mitchell Sextet
1966
Delmark DS 408

Numbers 1 & 2
Lester Bowie
1967
Nessa N1

Conglipitious
The Roscoe Mitchell Art Ensemble
1968
Nessa N2

1967/68
Art Ensemble Of Chicago
1967
Nessa N3

People in Sorrow
Art Ensemble Of Chicago
1969
EMI Pathe 2C062 10523

Message to Our Folks
Art Ensemble Of Chicago
1969
Actual BYG 529 328

Reese and the Smooth Ones
Art Ensemble Of Chicago
1969
Actual BYG 529 329

Jackson in Your House
Art Ensemble Of Chicago
1969
Actual BYG 529 302

Paris Session
Art Ensemble Of Chicago
1969
Arista Freedom

Tutankhamen
Art Ensemble Of Chicago
1969
Black Lion

Eda Wobu (bootleg)
Art Ensemble Of Chicago
1969
JMY

Certain Blacks
Art Ensemble Of Chicago
1970
America 30 AM 6098

Les Stances à Sophie
Art Ensemble Of Chicago
1970
EMI Pathe CO62 11365

With Fontella Bass
Art Ensemble Of Chicago
1970
America 6117

Live in Paris, Parts 1 & 2 (bootleg)
Art Ensemble Of Chicago
1970

Phase One
Art Ensemble Of Chicago
1971
America 30 AM 6116

Baptizum
Art Ensemble Of Chicago
1972
Atlantic SD 1639

Live at Mandel Hall
Art Ensemble Of Chicago
1972
Delmark 0432

Chi-Conga
Art Ensemble Of Chicago
1973
Paula LPS 4001

Fanfare for the Warriors
Art Ensemble Of Chicago
1973
Atlantic 90046

Kabalaba
Live at Montreaux
Art Ensemble Of Chicago
1974
AECO

Spiritual
Art Ensemble Of Chicago
1974
Polydor

Great Black Music
Art Ensemble Of Chicago
1978
Affinity

Nice Guys
Art Ensemble Of Chicago
1978
ECM LC 2516

Live in Berlin (bootleg)
Art Ensemble Of Chicago
1979
West Wind 2051

Full Force
Art Ensemble Of Chicago
1980
ECM 1 1167

Urban Bushmen
Art Ensemble Of Chicago
1980
ECM 1211/121 2641211

Among the People (bootleg)
Art Ensemble Of Chicago
1984
Praxis CJ103

Third Decade
Art Ensemble Of Chicago
1984
ECM 1273

Complete Live in Japan
Art Ensemble Of Chicago
1984
DIW

Naked
Art Ensemble Of Chicago
1984
DIW 8011

Ancient to the Future
Art Ensemble Of Chicago
1987
DIW

Art Ensemble of Soweto
Art Ensemble Of Chicago
1989
DIW CD 837 DIW LP 8038

Alternate Express
Art Ensemble Of Chicago
1989
DIW 832

Live at the Eighth Tokyo Music Joy
Art Ensemble Of Chicago
1990
DIW 842 E

Dreaming of the Masters: John Coltrane
Art Ensemble Of Chicago
1991
DIW 854

America South Africa
Art Ensemble Of Chicago
1991
DIW CD 848E

Dreaming of the Masters:
Thelonious Monk
Art Ensemble Of Chicago
1992
DIW 846E

About The Author

Writer, musician, poet, and lecturer, Lincoln T. Beauchamp, Jr., who is also known in the world of music as Chicago Beau, has been a friend and a creative associate of the Art Ensemble of Chicago for thirty years. He has collaborated with them musically on recordings [*Certain Blacks* 1970], and concert tours.

His personal discography spans thirty years and includes over twenty recordings of Blues, Jazz, and other musics as leader or accompanist with luminaries Archie Shepp, Philly Joe Jones, Cal Massey, Jeanne Lee, Pinetop Perkins, Billy Boy Arnold, Sunnyland Slim, Memphis Slim, Julio Finn, E. Parker McDougal, Anthony Braxton, Willie Kent, Jimmy Dawkins, Famoudou Don Moye, and others. He is presently touring with his band, Chicago Beau and His House Rockers.

He is founding editor of multi-arts journals, *Literati Chicago*, *Literati Internazionale*, and the *Original Chicago Blues Annual*. Among his published works are a collection of poems, interviews, articles and essays, titled, *Blues Stories;* and he has contributed articles and poetry to several magazines in Europe and the United States including the *Black American Literature Forum*, published by Indiana State University. He is an advisory editor to *Drumvoices*, a multi-arts journal published by Southern Illinois University, Edwardsville. A work-in-progress, *The Book of Blues Realities*, is to be published in February 1999.

The Contributors

DonAlonzo Beauchamp, son of Lincoln T. Beauchamp, Jr., has been working with the AEC since 1993. He is a record and music video producer; he has produced CDs of Blues, Hip Hop, and Jazz, including members of the AEC Malachi Favors Maghostut, and Famoudou Don Moye.

Hartmut Geerken is a writer and Jazz archivist. Among his major works is a complete discography, autobiography of Sun Ra titled, *Sun Ra Omniverse*.

Isio Saba is a promoter, writer, photographer, who has been associated with the AEC for twenty-five years. He resides in Rome, Italy.

Kalamu Ya Salaam is former Executive Director New Orleans Jazz and Heritage Festival. He is also a an internationally respected poet and author. His latest book titled *Reclaiming the Black Blues Self*, is published by Third World Press, Chicago.

Mike Hennessey is a Jazz pianist and writer. He has published a book on drummer Kenny Clarke, titled *Klook*, published by Quartet Books, London.

Photo Credits

Inside front cover, Erin Fahey
Page 2, AEC Archive
Page 3, Isio Saba
Page 6, Isio Saba
Page 7, Isio Saba
Page 8, Isio Saba
Page 12, Isio Saba
Page 13, DonAlonzo Beauchamp
Page 14, Deborah Bowie
Page 19, Isio Saba
Page 20, Jacques Bisceglia
Page 21, Jacques Bisceglia
Page 22, Isio Saba
Page 26, AEC Archive
Page 29, AEC Archive
Page 31, Luisa Cairati
Page 33, Guido Harari
Page 34, Marcel Zuercher
Page 48, H. Fruhof
Page 50, Isio Saba
Page 52, Kathy Sloan
Page 57, Isio Saba
Page 58, Leni Sinclair
Page 68, Isio Saba
Page 79, AEC Archive
Page 80, Jacques Bisceglia
Page 82, F. Harcourt
Page 88, Isio Saba
Page 104, Isio Saba
Back cover: Isio Saba

INDEX

'Don't Mess Up a Good Thing,' 40
'Rescue Me,' 40
11th Airborne Division Band, 70
7th Army Band, 71
Association for the Advancement of Creative Musicians, AACM,
24, 28, 40, 72, 73, 85
Abraham Lincoln Center, 71
Abrams, Muhal Richard 9, 24, 40
Ajaramu, 24, 61
Alan, Selah
Ali, Muhammad, 15, 29, 62
Allen, Marshall, 63
Allen, Selah, 61
Amabutho Zulu Male Chorus, 11, 65
America/South Africa US of A/ U of SA, 65
American Center of Paris, 29, 81
Anderson, Fred, 61, 72, 73,
Anderson, Marian, 30
Areski, 75
Arnold, Billy Boy, 9
Arnold, Charles, 63
Art Ensemble Of Soweta, 65
As If It Were The Seasons, 62
Atiba, 61
Atlantic Records, 62
Baker, Mickey, 81
Banha, Pedro
Baptizm, 30, 62, 98
Barker, Thur, 73
Barra, Beppe, 85
Barry, Fred, 28
Bass, Fontella, 9, 40
Beau, Chicago, 90
Beauchamp, DonAlonzo, 5, 63, 91
because, it's, this, dim, 24
Bell, Kelvyn, 65
Benevolent Paternal Order of the Elks, 53
Berry, Chuck, 36
Bibbs, Hart Leroy, 81
Bishop, Elvin, 25
Black Artists Group, BAG, 60,
    Bowie, Joe
    Carrol, Bakida
    Hemphil, Julius
    Lake, Oliver
    Le Flore, Floyd
    Menelek, Ajule
    Shaw, Bobo
    Thigpen, Bensid
Blackburn, Darlene, 61
Bluiet, Hamiett, 62
Blythe, Arthur, 64
Bowie, Bahnamous, 91
Bowie, Joe, 65
Brandon, Joel, 61
Brass Fantasy, 44, 53, 65, 86
Braxton, Anthony, 23, 40, 81
Brazzi, Francesca, 64
Brazzy Voices, 65
Broome, Marva, 81
Brown, Ari, 61, 94
Brown, James, 30, 54
Brown, Pepe, 29
Buckner, Thomas, 24
Burell, Kenny, 53
Butler, Jerry, 46
Butterfield, Paul, 25, 29
Cann, Elaine and Marty, 63
Carpentier, Alejo, 81
Carr, Ian, 83
Central State University, 54
Chat que Peche, 29, 81
Cherry, Don, 64
Chess Records, 40
Church of God in Christ, 27
Clark, Charles, 73, 89
Clarke, Kenny, 10, 64
Cole, Nat King, 70
Coleman, Ornette, 22, 30, 75
Coltrane, John, 12, 30
Congliptious, 25, 83
Cordell, Lucky, 9
Cosey, Pete, 61
Cotton, PC, 61
Creative Arts Collective of Detroit, 23
Crescendo, 11, 75
Crowder, Robert, 83
Cruz, Emilio, 60
Culloz, Maurice, 94
Cummings, John, 65, 95
cummings, e.e., 24
Cummins, Bob, 62

101

Cyrille, Andrew, 64
Daniele, Pino, 85
Darlene Blackburn Dancers, 61
Daughters of the Eastern Star, 53
Davis, Rahm Lee, 61
Davis, Richard, 64
de Johnette, Jack, 64, 71
de Piscopo, Tullio, 85
de Visscher, Philippe, 63
Defunkt, 65
Delaney, Beauford, 81
Delcloo, Claude, 28
Delmark Records, 62, 73
Detroit Free Jazz, 54
Deustche Kammerphilharmonie, 65
Diddley, Bo, 9
DIW, 64, 84
Dixon, Willie, 9
Dolphy, Eric, 22
Domino, Fats, 53
Dreaming of the Masters, 11, 12
Dyett, Captain Walter, 70
Earth, Wind, and Fire, 40
Echols, Rod, 63
ECM, 63, 64
Fanfare for Warriors, 62
Favors, Elder P. R., 27
Fielder, Alvin, 28
Finn, Julio, 81
Fletcher, Art, 54
Fontaine, Bridgitte, 10, 75, 95
Foreman, George, 62
Freeman, Chico, 62, 63, 64
Freeman, Von, 27, 72
Friend, Becky, 74
From the Roots to the Source, 86
Full Force, 11, 84
Gabrielle, Fausta, 64
Gaddie, Christopher, 73
Ganouhas, 55
Garrett, Raphael Donald, 71
Geerken, Hartmut, 5, 89, 100
Gianmarco, Maurizio, 85
Gilmore, John, 64
Gordon, Dexter, 81
Gravenitis, Nick, 25
Green, Grant, 53

Griffin, Johnny, 81
Hamilton, Chico, 28
Harris, Eddie, 61, 71
Hart, Billy, 94
Harting, Joe, 63
Hemphil, Julius, 62
Hennessey, Mike, 5, 83, 100
Hodges, Johnny, 22
Holmes, David, 63
India Navagation Records, 62
Jackson, John, 61
Jackson, Mahalia, 30, 53
Jenkins, Leroy 23
Jones, Philly Joe, 29, 64
Jordon, Clifford, 81
Kahil El Zabar, 24
Kahn, Chaka, 28
Kalamu Ya Salaam, 5, 15
Kalaparusha, 61
Kewu, 61
King, Albert, 39
King, B.B., 53
Kirk, Rashaan Roland, 30
Klienschmidt, Gabriele, GKP, 65
Koester, Bob, 62
Koran, Phil, 72, 95
Kubera, Joseph, 24
Lacy, Steve, 60
Les Stances à Sophie, 11, 60, 75
Lightsey, Kirk, 64
Lincoln University, 38
Lock, Graham, 83
Lytell, Johnny, 53
Mabon, Willie, 81
Magek, Evod, 61
Manoogian, Vartan, 24
Mason, Senior Bishop Charles Harrison, 27
McBee, Cecil, 64
McCall, Steve, 24, 74
McDuff, Brother Jack, 53
McGriff, Jimmy, 53
Melis, Marcello, 85
Meyers, Amina Claudine, 65
Mikller, Ron, 54
Mobley, Hank, 81
Moore, Charles, 59
Muhammad, Ameen, 63

Murolo, Roberto, 85
Murry, Atuque Harold, 61
Mwanga, Kunle, 60, 63
Nessa Records, 83
New York Organ Ensemble, 65
Nice Guys, 84, 85
North Texas State, 39
O'Gilvey, Victor, 63
Odwalla, 92, 96
Onisemoh, Kudus, 63
Outward Visions, 63
Oye, 61
Parker, Charlie, 30, 70
Potts, Steve, 12, 94
Powell, Tom, 54
Pryor, Anne, 63
Pullen, Don, 62
Pythod Club, 53
Rasa Artists, 63
Rashiek, Luba, 61
Robeson, Paul, 30
Robinson, Clifton, 61
Rolling Stones, 44
Rope-a-Dope, 62
Roscoe Mitchell Art Ensemble, 83
Roscoe Mitchell Ensemble, 73
Roots to the Source, 44
Ruiz, Hilton, 64
Saba, Isio, 64, 100
Sain, Oliver, 36, 39
Sainte Leu la Forêt, 41, 74
Salis, Antonello, 85
Salut, Michele, 63
Sarte, Jean Paul, 81
Savage, Pablo, 81
Senese, James, 85
Senghor, Leopold, 81
Serious Productions, 65
Sharock, Sonny, 81
Shepp, Archie, 28, 64, 81
Shango Njoko, 61
Silas, Meshach, 61
Silva, Alan, 74
Sinclair, John, 59
Sklar, Bob, 54
Slim, Memphis, 28, 73, 81
Smith, Bessie, 30
Smith, Leonard, (Tavanamuh, Falah), 25

Stevenson, Larry, 63, 77
Sompa, Titos, 55
Sound, 25, 62, 83
Spann, Pervis, 9
Storyville, 81
Stowsand, Thomas, 63
Studio Rivbea, 62
Sura, 61
Sun Ra All Stars, 64
Sun Ra, 10, 18, 64
Tatum, Art, 30
Taylor, Cecil, 11, 65
Tenores di Bitti, 85
Tharpe, Sister Rosetta, 27
The Leaders, 53, 64
Threadgill, Henry, 71, 72
Tiamo, 91
Tin Palace, 62
Turre, Steve, 65
Ujibkum Chariot, 65
Urban Bushmen, 64
Urbani, Massimo, 85
USS United States, 73
Waldron, Mel, 29, 94
Ward, Val Grey, 61
Waters, Muddy, 9, 30
Wayne, Jesus, 61
Wayne State University, 54, 59
Webster, Ben, 22
Weston, Randy, 55
White, Maurice, 40
Williamson, Enoch, 63
Wilmer, Valerie, 84
Wilson Junior College, 22, 71
Wilson, Jackie, 40, 41, 46
Wilson, Phillip, 25, 29, 59
Wood, Willie, 61
Wolcot, Colin, 63
Wolf, Howlin, 9
Wolliaston, Elsa, 55
Wright, Reverend Frank, 29, 81
Young, John, 61
Young, Lester, 70
Zigfield, 64
Zoot Suits, 70

Villa Tiamo
San San, Port Antonio, Jamaica, 1996

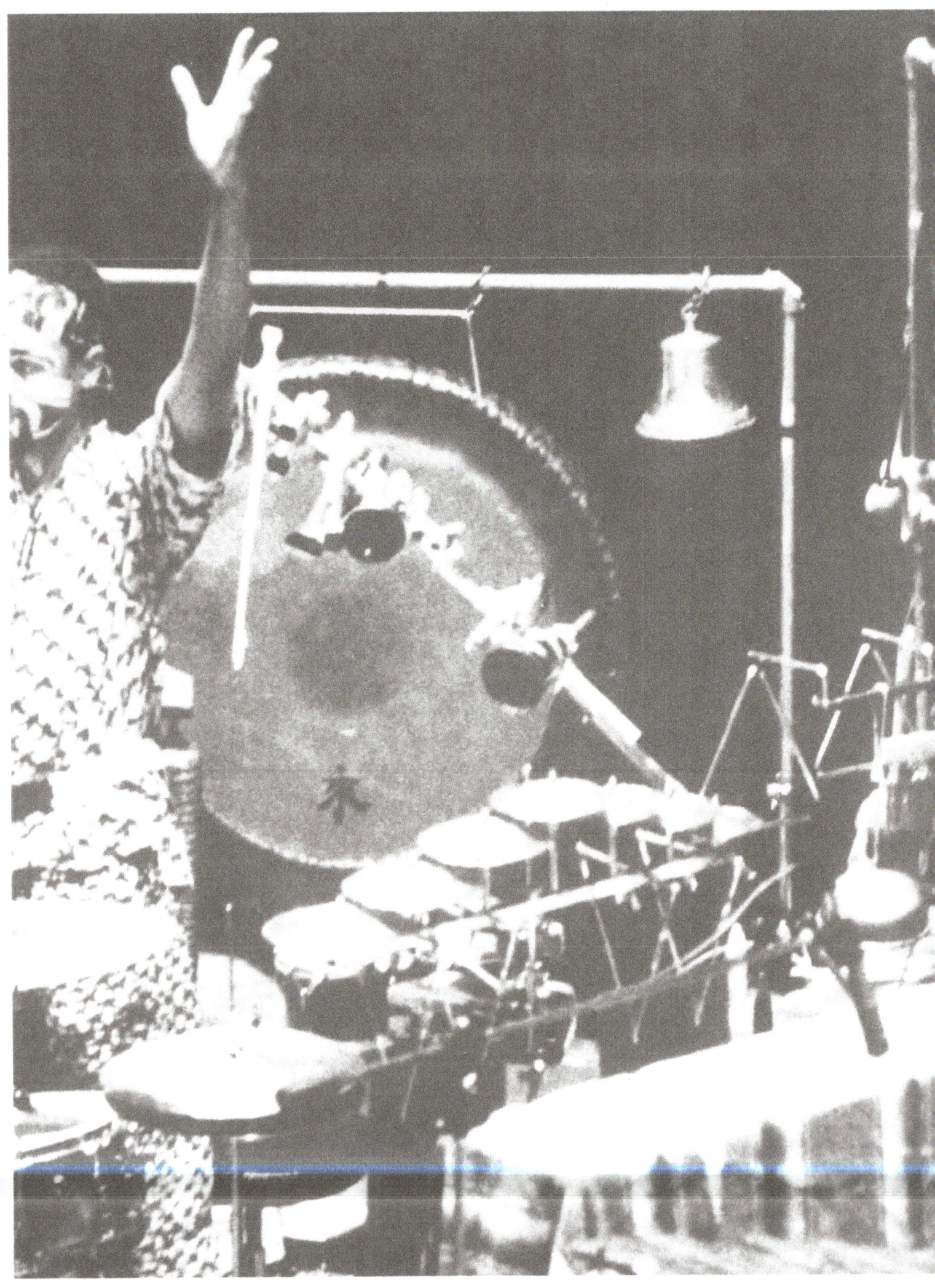

www.ingramcontent.com/pod-product-compliance
Lightning Source LLC
Chambersburg PA
CBHW061813290426
44110CB00026B/2864